perfect pitch

perfect pitch

3) men and women

EDITED BY
SIMON KUPER and
MARCELA MORA Y ARAUJO

review

First published in softback in 1998
by HEADLINE BOOK PUBLISHING

A REVIEW softback

10 9 8 7 6 5 4 3 2 1

ISBN 0 7472 7510 6

Typeset by
Letterpart Limited, Reigate, Surrey
Printed and bound in Great Britain by
Mackays of Chatham PLC, Chatham, Kent

HEADLINE BOOK PUBLISHING
A division of Hodder Headline PLC
338 Euston Road
London NW1 3BH

contents

acknowledgements

Thanks to Richard Adams, Gary Blumberg, Paddy Breathnach, Tomaso Capuano, Robert Chote, Giles Constable, Kevin Cummins, Dana Ferguson, Loui Fish, Leonie Gombrich, Arran Henderson, Simon and Martin Luke, Fiona McMorrough, Rana Mitter, Juan Mora y Araujo, Wolfgang Münchau, Matthijs van Nieuwkerk, Vivienne Schuster, Alex Skorecki, Michael Thompson-Noel and Robert Walpole, and to Ian Marshall and his colleagues at Headline.

Submissions to *Perfect Pitch* are welcome. These should be accompanied by a stamped, self-addressed envelope and sent to: The Editors, Perfect Pitch, c/o Headline Book Publishing, 338 Euston Road, London, NW1 3BH.

introduction

SIMON KUPER and MARCELA MORA Y ARAUJO

Perfect Pitch is a difficult journal, intended only for intellectuals. If you have read this far and understood all the words, you are to be congratulated. *Félicitations. Gratuliere. Gefeliciteerд*.

This third issue is about a subject that only intellectuals care about: men and women. A subject so complex that it can be dealt with only in long sentences. Crisp prose is no use.

That is because this issue sets out to say something that no one has ever said before. Namely, that the commercialisation of football post-Gazza's tears has ruined football. The game's traditional working-class support, which had revelled in the dodgy perms of the 1970s, has made way for the middle classes, women and trapeze artists who have jumped on the bandwagon of the media's feeding frenzy. You read it here first.

Do not look for good writing in this issue. Amy Raphael, Harry Ritchie, Joseph O'Connor, Liz Crolley and Gabriel Batistuta do not care about good writing.

Nor do Hugo Borst or Guus van Holland. What they set out to do – in Dutch – is write sociological tracts for graduate students. In this issue we have translated their texts. In future issues we may not.

Nor are the drawings by Paul Davis and Gordon Henderson intended to be amusing.

Lastly, the fact that *Perfect Pitch* is devoted to football is sheer chance. Had kitchen knives or the Tory Party been the fashion of the moment, we would have produced a magazine about them.

stevie macca: local hero

AMY RAPHAEL

Rock 'n' roll star

One minute we're having lunch in a nouveau English restaurant, the next we're running through Liverpool town centre dodging shoppers, giggling like schoolkids, clutching a stolen video signed by Robbie Fowler. Only it's not really stolen, Fowler gave it to us; we just forgot to pay. The alarms are ringing, louder and louder, but we don't look back. I am a little scared, but Steve McManaman is blasé. 'No one will stop me,' he says, laughing. He at least knows he could run all day.

We have left Fowler sitting at a small table in Virgin Records, sulking and forcing smiles at the Liverpool fans, at the hundreds of red shirts, each one of whom is desperate for him to sign his 'best goals' video. It is obvious that he would rather have been round the corner at the Lyceum, having lunch with Stevie Macca, his best mate.

Although adrenaline makes us want to keep running, we are constantly stopped by fans who ask McManaman to sign receipts, teen pop magazines, scraps of paper, whatever they can find in their pockets. Today he would like to think he is incognito (his Polo baseball cap pulled down, his Armani jacket collar pulled up), but there is no fooling the fans. And although perhaps two dozen stop him, some even wanting photos, he doesn't stop smiling. Not once.

Finally, we reach a pub. Inside it is warm and the beer is cold. I put away the video, with its scrawled, sarcastic message:

'Thanks for lunch.' McManaman says that Robbie will join us, probably sooner rather than later. A small group of men appears. One is Robbie's dad, a pleasant bloke who seems at ease with his son's fame and wealth. Proud, yes, but with no apparent interest in enjoying his son's success by proxy. Another is George Scott, a tough Glaswegian who acts as Fowler's accountant and manager. The third is younger and McManaman introduces him as Gordon, one of his best mates.

McManaman orders a round of beer and the talk is small. The previous day, Liverpool beat Arsenal 4-2 in the fourth round of the Coca-Cola Cup and there were, of course, celebrations. McManaman stayed up late, having a drink or two with Robbie and a *Times* journalist (McManaman has been writing a weekly column for the paper for the past few seasons).

'I'm lucky because I've always been dead skinny and I can eat what I want.' And the hangover this morning after a night of success and excess? 'I was up at eight running around the training ground in the fog. By nine, my head was clear.'

Two beers into the afternoon, Fowler turns up. He still looks miserable. 'You should be pleased, mate,' chides McManaman. 'This morning you convinced yourself no one would turn up and you'd be sitting there on your own feeling stupid. I told you you were being paranoid. How many videos did you sign? Three hundred? More? Just think of all that money!'

The afternoon passes. McManaman feeds the jukebox (Oasis, Radiohead, Space) while Fowler goes virtual skiing. Training each day between 10 a.m. and 12.30 p.m., they have afternoons to fill. Sometimes McManaman sees his former school mates or maybe he will sit in a quiet room in his flat on the Albert Dock and read (Ben Elton, Stephen Fry, Howard Marks). But only if there is 'total, total silence'; otherwise, he can't concentrate.

Occasionally the whole team go horse racing, spending

thousands of pounds and not really caring if they win it back. McManaman has a long-term girlfriend but she is in Germany studying law, so he is only distracted by her during university holidays. A couple of times a month, he will drive, very fast, to Manchester and go shopping. Liverpool's town centre has been reborn, with bars, restaurants and clubs opening every other week, but still there is no Armani, no Donna Karan.

It is dark outside and people drifting into the pub ask McManaman and Fowler for autographs. They don't mind, but it means chat is interrupted. Someone suggests food. It seems better than eating salt and vinegar crisps. A few minutes later, we stand outside the pub wondering where to go. No one wants to go upmarket, so we go to a pasta chain. We stand by the 'please wait here to be seated' sign and the banter continues. McManaman and Fowler are laughing at something Gordon's said. The manager appears, looking stern.

We are too raucous; we won't be given a table. McManaman and Fowler laugh even harder: they *aren't* turned away from restaurants in their home town. But there is no fuss. After all, there are dozens of places to eat now in Liverpool.

A short walk and we find ourselves sitting in a Greek taverna. Hundreds of photos form a collage on the walls and a crackly tape plays at full volume. There is no one else in the place. I realise that it's too late to get a train back to London and McManaman suggests I stay at the Moat House. I phone; they are fully booked. 'Here, give us your mobile,' says Fowler. 'I'll sort you out.' He phones; suddenly a room is available.

We eat moussaka and chips and drink fizzy water. Fowler rocks on the back two legs of his chair and tells silly stories; tears run down McManaman's face. Fowler is Liam Gallagher to McManaman's more controlled, thoughtful Noel.

At 9.30 p.m. it's time to go. McManaman takes me to the

Moat House to make sure everything is okay with the room. I ask him if he will suffer in the morning at training. 'I've only had a few beers. I'll get up at 7 a.m. and run them off. No problem.'

I am woken in my hotel room in what feels like the middle of the night by a noise which initially sounds like bullets being fired at my door. I realise it's a frenzied knocking sound. 'Robbie! Robbie! Come and see us,' a teenage girl's voice squeals. Robbie? 'Robbie Fowler! We know you're in there!' He's not, I assure them. After a while, they go away.

Truly, madly, deeply

Steve McManaman was born in Liverpool on 11 February 1972. Like Robbie Fowler and Michael Owen, he grew up an Everton fan; his father used to carry him into Goodison Park over the turnstiles when he was too small to walk through. Like any footballer, McManaman will tell you that he kicked a ball around as a toddler, but at junior school he was a top-class distance runner who collected a mantelpiece full of trophies and who beat Olympic track star Curtis Robb. It is a skill he never lost.

After years cleaning John Barnes' boots as an apprentice, McManaman signed up for Liverpool in 1990, making his full debut against Oldham Athletic in August 1991. He impressed with his energy, his pace (he can run non-stop for ninety minutes and still smile), his old-fashioned dribbling and his pleasant temperament. With his constant talk on the field, he could now even be captain in Paul Ince's absence.

He has his critics too. Being the first local lad since Sammy Lee to become a long-term regular after working his way through the junior ranks, the Koppites have high expectations of him. There are those who think he should have gone to Barcelona halfway through the 1997-98 season because he is past his best: he creates chances but he can't be relied upon to finish; he doesn't tackle; he surrenders possession too frequently. Perhaps the criticism would die down if Liverpool were to win the League . . .

The press, however, give him an easy enough time. Despite the 'Spice Boys' tag awarded Liverpool following accusations of wild social events taking preference to good old-fashioned hard graft, he has never appeared on the front page of the *News Of The World*. More importantly, in March 1998, Henry Winter of the *Daily Telegraph* referred to McManaman as 'one of the most skilful footballers in the English game' and went on to point out what we all know: that he has not imposed himself for England the way he does for Liverpool simply because Glenn Hoddle plays him out of position (as a wing-back instead of as an attacking midfielder).

Steve McManaman is bright, but – unlike Graeme Le Saux – he hasn't contrived an image which suggests he reads the *Guardian* in bed while sipping a cup of Earl Grey. But he is more than street sharp: he talks *and* listens (rare for celebrities); he reads (comedy, novels and sport; he is passionate about most sports) and writes (a half-ghosted column for *The Times* and articulate, considered pieces all on his own for *Esquire*).

He has the salary, the celebrity, the designer labels and the unnecessarily flash-around-town car but what is most important about Steve McManaman is this: he hasn't rejected his roots. He is proud of being a Scouser.

When I first met him back in November 1996, Steve McManaman had just bought a house in Crosby and, for the first time in his life, was preparing to move away from Kirkdale and Walton. 'I've got a place in the Docks, but I still stay at Mum and Dad's. They've got a little terraced house five minutes from Goodison. I don't get any problems living around there. To be honest, with my girlfriend studying in Germany, I'd rather stay with Mum and Dad. I'd rather have the conversation. I much prefer their company to my own. Oh yeah, and I've just bought them a house in Crosby.'

In March 1998, I convince McManaman to take me on a tour of Liverpool – his Liverpool. I am wondering if the McManaman who now lives in Crosby has changed. Where does Stevie Macca socialise and who with?

In a city which is still relatively poor despite its improved city centre, money stands out. Are childhood mates still around? Is it enough to be a nice bloke? Over in Manchester, David Beckham had one of his flash cars torched and a bullet engraved with his name sent through the post.

At 11.30 a.m. on Sunday, Steve McManaman turns up at the Moat House to pick me up. He is casually dressed: Polo T-shirt and baseball cap, dark denim jeans which look more Armani than Levi's. He orders a coffee and buys *News Of The World* for himself and, strangely, the *Mail On Sunday* for me. He reads his paper from back to front, first match reports and then gossip. 'Can you believe the Barça v Real Madrid score? It was 0-0 at half-time, I went into the kitchen to put my Chinese takeaway onto a plate and when I got back into the living-room, it was 3-0 to Barça. What a game. Incredible . . . Sophie Anderton's overdose. Due to stress and pressure. What's she on about? She dated the richest man in the world and did a bra ad . . . Shall we go?'

His mobile rings. It's Tony from Armani in Manchester, asking if he's thinking of coming over to do some shopping. Players get ten to twenty per cent off clothing, explains McManaman.

When he pays for the coffee, McManaman notices he's only been charged for two instead of three. The waitress is shocked.

'Gosh, you're an honest lad, aren't you?' He smiles.

His car, an 8-series laser blue BMW, is parked in front of the Moat House. The Liverpool squad always spend the night in the hotel before home games and he always leaves his car there when he comes into town. Not because he thinks some Scouser might nick the hubcaps, but because it's convenient.

In the car there is no rubbish or mess, just a fake moustache. 'My younger brother, who's seventeen, gave it to me. I have it in every new car I buy. The stickiness has worn off now, but I worry if it's not there. It's like a lucky mascot. My brother's not remotely interested in football, you know. It's cool because it'd be tough on him if he wanted to be a footballer too. He's so bad he doesn't know what his school mates are on about when they say "your brother was terrible yesterday". He came to a game once last season because Mel C had asked me for a ticket and he was desperate to meet a Spice Girl. So I got him a ticket too and he took a book along to read! *And* I scored two goals!'

We drive from town to Kirkdale. Radiohead's current album, *OK Computer*, is on the car stereo, but so low you can barely hear Thom Yorke's pained vocals.

'This is where I'm originally from. That was the first Astro-turf pitch to be laid in the area and lots of us used to play on it. My main haunt used to be Kirkdale Community Centre; I was there every night after school. My Nanna lives in that house just there; it's sheltered accommodation. I see her all the time. She's getting old now, so we bring her up to our house a lot.' He slows the car down by a terrace of two up and two down houses. 'This is my first house. Number 45 Orwell Road. See those railings? We were the first to have little railings. My mates all lived round here too. One of them actually lives in a bungalow round the corner. He rents it off another mate.' He points to a pub. 'My mates could be in there. What time is it? Not yet midday? Perhaps it's a bit early yet.'

We come first to a Catholic church, the one he used to attend regularly until he stopped going for some reason he's not sure of, and then to a school building. It is small, with a tiny playground, few trees, hardly any grass: nowhere to kick a ball around. 'My junior school,' McManaman says with pride. 'St John's. My Dad went there before me. We used to play football in the yard. It was just about possible. Before the local derby one year, we had a Liverpool v Everton game for the kids and it was broadcast on Sky Sports. It was cool – all the kids were going mad!'

I am curious: did he really stand out at junior school? There is no arrogance in his reply. 'Yeah. When I was seven, I used to play with the nine- and ten-year-olds.' He laughs. 'I was *really* small. I've always been thin, but back then I was thin *and* tiny. Can we drive up here? I'm not sure, but what the hell. There's no one around. This is the local park where I used to play all the time as well. It's a gravel pitch. It's rack and ruin now. You'd get to school at 8.30 a.m. and play for half an hour; then at morning break, dinner time, afternoon break. It was literally football, football, football. I used to do cross-country running at junior school; I was very good at that. But, to be honest, I never really enjoyed it. It was a one-man sport so it wasn't my thing.'

Was he a popular lad at school? Again, there is no hesitation. 'Yeah.'

Then a pause.

'I don't know.'

He laughs.

'Probably. I was always a nice lad. I was always good at school. I was always very bright. But I was popular too, I suppose because I played football. I never picked on anyone, I was never a bully. To be honest, the five or six mates I had then are still around.'

Are they threatened by your success? 'I don't think so. They're thrilled. They come to every home game and they'll travel as far as Birmingham, to see us play Aston Villa.'

And the money, is that a problem? He frowns. 'No. No. My mates are cool. I see them all the time . . . We're driving from Kirkdale to Walton now. I used to live up this road.' The houses are bigger, semi-detached. The road is narrow and he drives slowly. 'We moved here when I was thirteen. And stayed until about sixteen months ago.' For a moment, he is pensive. 'This house was always great. I think we just moved in the end because we could. We are right near Goodison Park, but I never had any problems living here. When Everton used to play at home, people would park on both sides of the road and at times I had nowhere to park my own bloody car!'

The mobile rings. It's Gordon, the lad who turned up at the pub. 'Let's go and see him. He's not a school mate, but he's just bought a new house and I'd like to have a look.' We turn a few corners and park in a tiny dead end street. Two seven-year-old boys are kicking a ball around. McManaman disappears into a newly painted terraced house.

'Nice car, that,' says one of the boys, standing as close as he dare.

'Imagine how fast it goes,' adds the other, hugging the plastic ball to his chest.

Gordon appears with Steve to say hello. He is barefooted. 'I'll ring you after,' McManaman says. 'That old lady at the end of your road just said to me: "Next time you come down, bring us a memento." I said: "All right, love." '

Next stop, Crosby. On the way, I try to make him discuss his future. He will be honest only about Liverpool. 'I *love* it here. I love the fact that I was born here. Without a doubt. I must admit that I like going to London every now and then, but I love coming home. I always look forward to it.'

In the April 1998 issue of *FourFourTwo*, a journalist mentioned McManaman going into a shop and buying an Italian dictionary. Why? 'No one knows whether that was for me or if I was picking it up for a friend,' he says with a smile. 'But I think that everyone ought to have a second language.'

If you moved abroad, you'd really miss Liverpool, wouldn't you? 'Yeah. God, yeah. You see some of the foreign fellas who come to play for Liverpool. For the first few months, they live in a hotel, don't speak a word of English and have no mates. Not real ones.'

And yet at one point, you seemed on the verge of moving to Barça. 'When you look at the big European clubs on television, they've got a certain aura about them. I went to visit Incey in Italy at the end of last season, when he was leaving Inter and signing for us. He told me that the first year was hard, but after that he *loved* it. I think it was difficult for him to move back to England. He was missing out on the chance to play with Ronaldo! And with AC Milan having such a bad season now, it must be great at Inter.'

We reach the docks. I mention the time Fowler scored and lifted his shirt to reveal a T-shirt with a text supporting the striking Liverpool dockers. It was later reported that the T-shirt was initially McManaman's idea, but that Fowler agreed to wear it as he was more likely to score. 'Lots of my Dad's mates are dock workers. It wasn't a case of coming out and supporting them because it was the correct thing to do; I simply knew them, I used to have the occasional drink with them. I knew the predicament they were in and I wanted to give them support as friends. It wasn't a political act.'

He pauses, looking at the houses. They are big, detached.

There are two, maybe three new-looking cars in the driveways. 'This is a horrendously busy road because it's the only way to get through to Formby and Southport . . . and I live just off it. My road is nice and quiet. It's like living in the country but only ten minutes drive into town. I live there.'

He pulls up. Behind a tall hedge, at the end of a long driveway, is a pretty big detached house. At least three times the size of the one in Walton. 'To be honest, we don't know many people here. There's a little cricket club down the road but we haven't joined yet,' he says laughing. 'I've just got a house round the corner for my sister, who's a few years older than me. As she's got a sixteen-month-old baby, it's ideal because she brings it across every day. My Mum and Dad live for the little baby, really. So it's great.'

I want to have a look round the house, see how big his TV is, what his kitchen units are like. But I say nothing. I remember McManaman once saying how he was the only player who refused to let anyone from the official monthly Liverpool magazine go anywhere near his house. I say it must be great to live in an area where your neighbours either don't know who you are or are too rich to say anything. 'It is, although people who fail to be intimidated by the long drive still knock on the door. They ring the intercom, "Is Macca there?" My Mum or Dad says, "No, he's having a bath. Come back later when he's gone out!" '

We drive around Crosby, mostly for my benefit; I spent my childhood school holidays here with my grandparents. McManaman wonders how much of it I remember. It's been two decades and most of it is a blur. We end up at Crosby Baths, which I do remember, if only for the ridiculously high diving board. 'Me and my mates used to get the train out here to go swimming,' he says. 'Well, I say swimming; all I could do was paddle. I was terrible. Always stayed near the edge. You remember the 30ft diving board? There was a test. Those who could go up and dive straight off were dead cool. The rest of us weren't. I'd be standing up there for half an hour before I'd jump – and I only jumped then to save face.'

The phone rings again. It's someone from a local football team thanking him for donating a shirt. It turns out that McManaman gives away so many of his shirts for charity that he only has a few in the house, and one of those used to belong to his boyhood hero, Everton's maverick striker Duncan McKenzie. 'There are so many local charity events. There was an auction the other week. Razor [Neil Ruddock] and Robbie [Fowler] donated a pair of boots each. Razor's went for eight quid and Robbie's got seventy-five, I think. Robbie was worried whether to donate a pair he'd worn which had mud on them, or some which were unworn but clean. All my mates have got an England shirt each. Between them, they've got more than me.' He shakes his head in disbelief.

The most famous school in Crosby is Merchant Taylors, a grand private school. My grandmother always used to drive past it talking in a hushed voice, as though she wasn't worthy. McManaman's junior school encouraged him to take a scholarship exam for Merchant's, which he did. As far as he remembers, it wasn't the exams which caused a problem but the interview. In a predominantly rugby-playing school, the young Macca talked about what he knew: football. He wasn't accepted.

Fifteen years on, he has no regrets. 'There is no point in going to a school like that unless you intend to take A-levels and go to college. I knew that I wanted to take the risk of choosing football. I used to play for a schoolboy team in Penny Lane and when we were sixteen, six or seven of us were offered YTS schemes with Liverpool. It was great; we'd come in at nine o'clock and mix with the likes of John Barnes, Steve McMahon, Alan Hansen and Mark Lawrenson. Back then, they were the team which won everything. We'd clean up after them, train a bit ourselves and leave at two o'clock.'

Can you remember your first pay cheque? 'I think the YTS paid £27.35 a week, but Liverpool used to pay our lodgings as well. That was effectively for our Mums – I'd give mine a fiver – so that was up to £60-odd already. Then we'd get expenses as well, so of course I'd take twenty-seven buses to get to Anfield, which was within walking distance. The first year was around £60 to £65 a week and in the second year it went up by about a fiver.'

And when you turned professional? 'The first pro contract was £225 a week. It seemed like a lot back then; I suppose it still is. When Robbie Fowler turned pro, I think he got more than that. And Michael [Owen] got even more again.' There is a long pause, in which McManaman looks unusually serious.

Of course, McManaman is earning around £10,000 to £15,000 a week now (figures he won't confirm or deny). He's bought two big houses, he owns the laser blue BMW and he's just acquired an Aston Martin. Life is sweet. But what happens in, say, ten years' time, when he'll be forced to retire? He thinks management is too tough because football is spiralling out of control, but he's not sure he can play the game virtually every day of his life until he's thirty-five, thirty-six and then suddenly stop.

Already a rock 'n' roll star of sorts, he thinks music may be an option. 'Not singing, God bless us! Although I was in the school choir when I was younger, there is *no* chance of me singing. I love music though. Who knows, maybe I'll produce. Every kid in Liverpool wants to be a footballer or a rock star. And then . . . footballers love music and rock stars want to play football.'

Driving back towards Lime Street train station, there is an increasing number of boarded-up shops. Streets and streets of dilapidated buildings, smashed windows. There is no greenery, just greyness. 'I don't tend to think about it,' says McManaman with a shrug. 'As with any city, there are nice areas and not so nice areas. It just depends where you look. And where you live. We're back near Kirkdale now; it's where I used to live, so it's different for me really.'

For the fourth time in less than an hour on a Sunday afternoon, the phone rings. It is Paul Ince. He wants to know what's happening this evening. McManaman agrees to go out with him and team-mate Steve Harkness. A minute later, there's another call. 'All right. How are you man? I've just been driving past yours. I'm doing an interview. You're nosey, aren't you? If I tell you who with, you still won't know, like. Put you in? You're already in – I've just been talking about my childhood and my old mates from school. God bless us. Behave yourself. You just want to see your name in print. Okay, I'll tell her some real big lies: tell her what a nice lad you are. I'll give you a ring later. See you after. Ta ra.'

Stevie Macca smiles: 'It's great having real mates. Really great.'

I have no more questions.

It's the real thing

On 25 April 1998, Liverpool play Chelsea at Stamford Bridge. I go to the game with the Lightning Seeds' Ian Broudie. It is a glorious spring day and we go to the ground early. The Liverpool players are warming up; David James has just become a bottle blond again and Robbie Fowler is sitting in the dugout, his crutches at his side. His face isn't visible, but his hair, glistening with gel, identifies him.

There is a sudden surge of Liverpool fans to the front of the lower stand, just to the left of the dugout. It's Steve

McManaman, who's jumped over the advertising hoarding to sign autographs. He stands there patiently for five whole minutes, signing programmes, tickets, shirts.

At one point, he looks up, squinting into the sun. He sees us and waves. 'I'll see youse two later. I'll get you into the Players' Lounge,' he says with a big grin.

Ian Broudie, who himself is signing programmes and tickets and thanking people for complimenting 'Three Lions', declares himself a McManaman fan. 'It'd be good to see him in a team with players as good as him around him, which is a bit of an indictment to the team, but you know . . . this season he's been really determined. He's tackling back. He's the kind of player who takes on responsibility.'

If he doesn't leave Liverpool, could he be captain? 'He'd make a great captain. He's the kind of player who keeps the vibe up and he talks non-stop. I've met him a few times after Lightning Seeds gigs and he's a decent bloke. It's hard for real Scousers to leave Liverpool. I should know; I only managed to move to London a few years ago and I miss it every day. And Steve's a bit of a local hero. But at the same time, I think he has the ability to be a great footballer on the world stage.'

More people arrive. By coincidence, Robbie Fowler's dad sits next to me. He wolf whistles his son, who sticks a thumb up in return. A grand-looking man in his seventies sits in front. Mr Fowler calls him 'H'. He looks strangely familiar. When Jamie Redknapp appears from the tunnel and 'H' talks about 'my boy', I realise it's Jamie's granddad and Harry's dad. He has chosen to watch Liverpool today rather than West Ham.

The game finishes 4-1 to Chelsea. It is raining hard. Ian and I hang around for a few minutes to see if McManaman appears and then we go to the pub. Everyone in the pub sings 'Three Lions' the second we walk in, so we drink outside, in the rain. My mobile rings during the second pint. It's McManaman. He wonders where we are. I wonder what happened in the game. He swears a bit and then starts laughing again.

'Sorry I missed you, mate,' he says when I pass the phone over to Ian. 'How's it going with Ian McCulloch? Is his World Cup record better than yours? Ha ha.'

Life gets sweeter every day

It is March 1998 and I am in the Players' Lounge at Anfield. Liverpool have just beaten Bolton 2-1 and the players are still in the bath. I want to share the moment with someone, tell them what it feels like to be standing here after all my childhood dreams. But the only person around is Robbie Fowler, who is leaning on a table at the far end of the room holding crutches.

This has been a heartbreaking season for Fowler. He will miss the chance to play in a World Cup. And the tabloids have not been kind – they accused him of demanding £50,000 a week, a rumour which has angered the fans, who in turn have embraced new striking superstar Michael Owen. And Robbie has just been told he probably won't play again until December 1998. At the earliest.

McManaman appears, hair wet and suit smart, and greets Fowler fondly. 'All right there, Cripple. How you doing? Heard you didn't get here till half time. What were you doing?'

Neil Ruddock, on the verge of signing for QPR, brings some bottles of beer over (Carlsberg Ice, of course, courtesy of Liverpool's shirt sponsors). 'This is Neil,' says McManaman. 'Don't call him Razor.' Ruddock mock smiles at McManaman and extends a hand wet with the coldness of the beer.

Two young boys who've been nudging each other finally ask McManaman if they can have their photo taken with him. He obliges, smiling. 'I'd better hide this bottle behind your head, mate. I can't be seen drinking beer . . . 'cause I'm sponsored by Absolut Vodka. Ha ha.'

Ruddock asks McManaman what his nicknames are. 'Macca. Stevie. Shaggy. It was Mouse at school. Something to do with a TV programme called *McMouse*. You know, McManaman; McMouse. Mouse. At one point, I was known as Legend. I don't know why. I don't! I bloody don't! Hey, Cripple, we're supposed to call you God, aren't we?' Fowler gives him a wry smile.

Jason McAteer is wearing a dark grey Seventies-style suit with trousers so flared you can't see his shoes. There are *sotto voce* jokes about shampoo ads; someone says he can't be earning enough if he has to do anti-dandruff ads and everyone sniggers loudly.

There is no sign of Michael Owen but Paul Ince is here and he is the only one not drinking beer; he is sipping chilled white wine, his little finger held away from the glass, an affectation he perhaps picked up in Milan.

Out of nowhere, a dozen or so young Japanese men appear. Clutching carrier bags advertising JD Sports and Sports Division, they ask Ruddock to take a photo of them with some other players. Razor holds the miniature state-of-the-art camera upside down, back to front. He pretends not to know which button to press. The fans are perplexed. They laugh nervously and try to show him what to do but he ignores their shaky English. Robbie Fowler drops a crutch and no one will pick it up until a Japanese fan offers. Finally, Fowler, McManaman, Ince and Jamie Redknapp pose for the picture, all pulling playground faces. The young Japanese men look deadly serious.

After an hour or so, McManaman has had enough. We try to leave by the back door, but before he can climb into his laser blue BMW, a hundred hungry Liverpool fans surround him. He signs as he walks, painstakingly writing his name time and again (he will later say: 'If you see other footballers' autographs, they're an absolute disgrace, they just go "whoosh" – but I'm fairly neat and my name's so long, so it takes ages'). He reaches the car, opens the door and the fans, boys and girls, but mostly boys, try to follow.

'That's it now,' he says. 'Can I shut my car door please?' They ignore him. 'Please, just sign this Macca. Please.' He sighs. This is strange; McManaman prides himself on being 'very, very, very relaxed all the time'. Yet here he is, almost at the point of gritting his teeth. The fans sense the tension and move away. McManaman immediately laughs. 'What a fuckin' nightmare! Can't even get into my own car.' The fans are left without autographs but still, they wave as we drive away from the ground.

At the Moat House, McManaman agrees to a few drinks. He's not staying out tonight; his girlfriend is studying at home for her law finals and he wants to go to his flat on the Docks to see her. There doesn't seem to be a drop in adrenaline levels following the game – our group expands constantly over the next couple of hours and McManaman's phone rings with alarming regularity. It's his girlfriend, asking what time he thinks he'll be back; it's 'Jamo' (David James) then 'Incey' (Paul Ince) then 'Arkers' (Steve Harkness), all wanting to know what's happening tonight.

Conversation jumps from one piece of gossip to another. McManaman fuels the rivalry between Liverpool and Manchester United by discussing the Neville brothers. 'They're *real* party animals, fuckin' hell! A pineapple juice for Gary and a lemonade for Philip.' Two business associates of Fowler's manager, George Scott, turn up and there is talk of Liverpool's recent friendly against Rangers at Ibrox. Talk, mostly, of Paul Gascoigne being out injured and behaving even more oddly than usual. McManaman wants to know if I have any football gossip and is disappointed when I only repeat things he already knows.

When the phone calls are all from his girlfriend, McManaman decides to leave. He sends me to Buro, a new restaurant where Robbie Fowler, his girlfriend of the moment, her best friend and George Scott are having dinner. There, I find Robbie sitting on the elevated level of the busy restaurant, wounded leg resting on a chair, king of all he surveys. He is in a good mood, but there is no real belly laughter. Because, of course, his best mate has gone home early.

nothing to play for

ROB NEWMAN

The same forces that have organised the factory and the office have organised leisure as well, reducing it to an appendage of industry. Accordingly sport has come to be dominated not so much by an undue emphasis on winning as by the desperate urge to avoid defeat . . . When sports can no longer be played with an appropriate abandon, they lose the capacity to raise the spirits of players and spectators, to transport them to a higher realm of existence. Prudence, caution and calculation, so prominent in everyday life but so inimical to the spirit of games, come to shape sports as they have shaped everything else.

The Culture of Narcissism, *Christopher Lasch*

Football's so joyless most of the time. Match officials now actually have instructions to stop players celebrating too much! I can't believe we just accept that. *Or* the day-glo, diddy-jacket stewards telling you not to jump up and down too much in the stands after a goal, and throwing you out for swearing even when a player is indeed playing like a cunt. This should be the other way round: there should be an automatic three-match ban for any player who asks a smiling fat bloke to leave after a pitch invasion. It's his team more than the player's. Who paid for the pitch anyway?

And where football's not plain joyless, it's neurotic. Everton getting all stressed and freaked end-of-season because they had to play with an orange ball. At school if you were good at football you were good at football even when it was a tennis ball on asphalt. England won the World Cup with an orange ball. But Everton were like Rain Man: *No, definitely a white ball, should definitely be a white ball. Uh-oh, orange wrong, orange wrong!*

Cesare Maldini looks like Iggy Pop, we've all noticed. But think about what that means for a second. Iggy Pop looks as craggy and raddled as that because he has taken every drug known to man, and did so for decades. Cesare Maldini just managed the Italian national squad for a couple of seasons.

I always envy foreign supporters. When PAOK Athens came to Arsenal their away contingent pogo-ed, sang and made merry for ninety minutes. Wimbledon–Middlesbrough at a foggy, cold Selhurst Park Sainbury's. All these Brazilians came to see Juninho. Beautiful women, handsome garments, cool tweed-age, flags, drums, trombones. They stopped and stared like a samba band at the Somme across the dismal pitch at fish-faced Palace fans mouthing silent curses in the sour mist.

Foreign fans have more fun. Apart from England, the only other country not to have a hundred-foot flag or silky banner passed overhead is the USA. This is because Anglo-Saxon capitalism does not encourage collective life; nothing is owned collectively ('Look, that's *my* hundred-foot flag, pass it back. Come on, please . . .'). No collective life is also why England fans are the only ones in the world reduced to singing the fucking National Anthem – of all things – at a game (France doesn't count because the 'Marseillaise' is a rebel song named after a town with a large immigrant population. An English equivalent might be the Clash's 'Guns of Brixton'.).

There has always been a struggle for the heart of football from its very birth. Association football – as opposed to football – was born shortly after capitalism. The spirit of early bourgeois society, Lasch says, was deeply antithetical to play. In *Dombey and Son* Dickens skits the early capitalist anti-play ethic when the upright Dombey refuses to call his new maid by her given name

Toodles as it is not sensible enough. So she has to be called Polly instead. The northern aldermen at Derby likewise insisted on chopping the 'e' off Paulo Wanchope, so it's just pronounced One-chop rather than the celebratory, carnival fiesta of the three-syllable 'Wanchope' (rhymes with Too-Rye-Aye) as this would have led to wantonness and lewdness. They were like Vic Reeves' Mr Dennis character who famously refused to stock Curly-Wurlies because he found them 'far too elaborate'.

Yes, part of this is to do with big business entering the game – 'bringing the game into disrepute', for example, just means upsetting advertisers, behaviour not conforming to product profile and target audience – but only part of it. Because it's not just the professional game.

I used to play on Sunday mornings on an all-weather pitch in Battersea, but I gave up because there was absolutely no sense of play. Seconds after kick-off otherwise likeable men became disgruntled, peevish PE teachers, always telling you off and saying 'get back', 'cover back', 'go to him'. I wanted to say 'Look, we're a bunch of thirty-year-old comedians, none of us can play, what does it matter?' When they said why didn't you head it?, I'd put on a pouffy voice and say that the ball was ever so hard and was falling out of the sky with a worrying velocity. Secretly, though, I thought that these men were revealing their true spirits and that if fascism ever came here, these would be the willing commissars, timetable clerks and neighbourhood spies.

Recently I've found a five-a-side where you don't get nagged and told off. A friend of mine organised mixed-sex games at Regent's Park where there are yellow cards for what she calls jargon, i.e., 'man on', 'to me', 'square ball' and red cards for machismo and moaning at team-mates.

Apart from these, the last game I really enjoyed was on a beach with Spaniards. With these campadres if you tried a mazey dribble or flamboyant, no-hope bicycle kick and it didn't come off, they didn't get on your case about it but applauded with cries of *'Bastardo puto!'* which is Catalan for bold ambition or nice idea, better luck next time, or simply bravo! And, unintimidated, I played the best I've ever played. Which led to mixed feelings as I realised that had I been born in France or Spain I would have ended up being a midfield general at Marseille or Barca. I wrote to Lancaster Gate on my return pointing out that if Zidane had been born in Hackney then he would have faced the ludicrous situation I faced in the English game of being last to be picked in the playground and once even substituted for a girl.

The next two and a half pages detail a vision of the sort of player I would almost certainly have been. So important is this to the current debate about the English game I feel certain they won't be cut.

NOTHING TO PLAY FOR

PERFECT PITCH

from the street to the pitch

GABRIEL BATISTUTA

A dark-coloured car changed my life. I was sixteen and head over heels in love with Irina. I had no real ambitions – study, leisure, cronies, that's what my life in Reconquista was like. Never could I have guessed that my life was going to take a different road. But many things were to happen before I actually saw that car parked in front of my house. Now that I come to think of it, there were many revealing signs, but they meant nothing to me at the time.

I remember my first football ground very well. It was us – the boys from the *barrio* Chapero – who built it on a barren, stony stretch of land wedged between the railway and a side road. Pulling up weeds and flinging turfs of red earth at the passing trains had been a sweat, and there was trouble every time someone tumbled down among the stones; our knees were scratched all over, but we were happy when we managed to save our trousers and shirts. How could we possibly go back home and tell our parents we had ripped our jeans? After setting the poles we named our little pitch 'Earthworm' because the ground was long and narrow. There was an argument before each and every game to decide whether the road was to be considered part of the football ground. If the road was to be included, then the ground measures became incredible – one corner was five paces from the goal, the other one about twenty. I was eleven years old, and that is where I played football for the first time; I was – no need to say it – a striker.

A few months later my first football team was born. We called ourselves the 'Merry Party' and our seat was the Tozzi brothers' house. We got along really well, me and the three Tozzi brothers: Marcelo, who was my age, Walter, who was the same age as my elder sister, and 'Boccia' (bowl), as we called the third brother. They had wonderful parents, considered the best in the area. I still meet the Tozzi brothers every time I go back to Reconquista; two of them work as haulage contractors, the other is a PE instructor, and he owns a gym.

Julio, the head of the Tozzi family, was a truck driver; in the summer he 'put' all of us kids in his truck, and off we went to explore Argentina. That's how I took my first holiday. Julio used to put some mattresses for us under the awning, and there we stayed, having a hell of a good time. When the truck was loaded – usually with hides, timber, or some sort of delicious biscuit – we climbed into the cab, Julio put the recess bed back into place, and the six or seven of us made the most incredible noise. My first trip with them was to Poscadas, the capital city of Missiones; the second one – horrible – was to Cordoba, where I broke my right foot. I was taken to a sort of faith-healer, who rubbed and twisted it for a long time. One week later I was back home, and my swollen foot was as big as a melon.

The 'Merry Party' took part in a tournament for the first time during a hot summer in Reconquista. I was twelve, and played centre forward. We played on the Cathedral ground, and I scored many goals, but was not placed first among the goal scorers because I was much younger than my adversaries. The year went by, with little glory and lots of fun. The following year, the 'Merry Party' resumed its activity; I scored many goals, our shirts were white and green, and number 9 – the number of a lifetime – was already on my back. Braida was still our coach, you could say he was the one who helped me with my first studded boots – literally. Luis was a shoemaker, and he let me work in his workshop. He even taught me how to sew shoes.

Braida had set up quite a nice little team. Piloti was our goalkeeper; we called him *'flaco'* (weed) because he was about 6ft 8in tall and skinny, or *'tenaglia'* (pincers) because he never dropped a ball. Then there was Fabio, Braida's eldest son, Marcelo Tozzi, Casanova and Tatu, a stout boy, and – last but not least – myself. The others called me Bati, or *'Gringo'* because of my fair hair, a rather unusual colour in my country. That tournament made our team well known all over the region, and the managers of some teams from Reconquista nagged my father because they wanted me to play for them. I had an offer from Telares, another one from the Racing club, and the third one from La Costa, my uncle Melchior's club. I ended up playing for Platense.

I was already sixteen years old but my father wouldn't let me sign a real contract because of some strange goings on. What some managers did was to make a young player sign a binding contract and then demand a lot of money to set him free, when an important team asked for him. My father realised before I did that football was going to be my career. He used to tell me: 'Maybe one day you'll decide to be a professional footballer and you'll find yourself bound.'

My father very rarely talked about soccer – it only happened a couple of times – and he never mentioned technical matters. When I was a boy, I was in the bad habit of getting angry with the referee and gesticulating: kids mimic the stars they see on TV. Dad told me not to do that. The second time he mentioned football was because he was angry with me and the rest of the team. We had spent all day at the swimming pool, and in the evening we were so tired we lost the football match; my father said to me: 'You must learn to respect what you do.'

When it came to certain subjects, my father was inflexible. That was clear even to the managers of Platense, who had a hard job persuading him. Or rather, it was he who persuaded the managers that the contract he had made up was the only one I would sign. That contract included all conceivable clauses: I had the right to leave the club whenever I wanted to, without having to pay a penalty. But in those days, I thought of everything but football. Platense football ground was about a quarter of a mile from where I lived, but it seemed to me to be far away, as if it were in some other town. My grandfather Nestor lived by the stadium; from his windows, he could see the pitch – a barren piece of ground with very little grass. I used to play up to two matches a day, one with the junior players, and one with the seniors. The coach of the junior team was called Reinoso, a quiet sort of fellow. He was the one who taught me to take pleasure from the game. Reinoso still trains the boys in Reconquista, and when I go back, I go and see him.

I played my first 'serious' match, when I was sixteen and a half. The opposing team – Racing – was the richest in Reconquista. I can still remember the score – 1-0 for Racing. That year was a gratifying one, because it gave me the possibility of measuring my strength against my uncle Melchior, who was still playing for La Costa. I had been preparing for that match for over a month, thinking about it night and day; I had even put a lot of enthusiasm into my training, but the day before the match I was taken ill. I had a temperature and a sore throat, but I kept mum. When I entered the field, I could barely stand; my uncle marked me man-to-man, and he beat me all along. When the match was over, I had to be lifted up bodily to be carried home, and had to keep to my bed for a week.

I was about to get my first pair of professional boots. I still know what boys feel when, in a sports shop, they set eyes on a pair of studded boots. That's exactly how I felt, when the management of Platense gave me my first pair. They were about two sizes too big. It was Friday, and we were supposed to play on the following day, so I stuffed my boots with cotton-wool and entered the field just the same. In my eyes, those boots were beyond price: they showed that Platense considered me a professional player. Unfortunately, after a couple of matches the boots were broken. They were so big that I dug a hole in the ground every time I kicked the ball.

That year I scored a lot. Whenever I come home, my mother always asked the same question: 'How many goals did you score?' You see, she didn't ask whether I had scored or not.

I enjoyed playing, but training meant torment to me. I argued with the coach all the time. The trainer gave me no rest; I was the youngest player in the team, and the older ones, who worked all day before their training, kept telling me I had to work harder and called me a slacker. But I had met Irina, so I only ran one lap round the field and then off I went to her house. One day the senior players got really angry. I had not trained all week long, but on Sunday I was picked for the team. 'If you let Batistuta play, we are going home,' they shouted to poor Sosa. There was a riot, but in the end I was allowed to play.

I played for Platense for two years; I felt at ease there. But not even when a big-shot in Argentine football turned up, did I realise that football was going to be my career. The guy's name was Jorge Griffa, and he was one of the most celebrated talent-scouts in the country. It was in a friendly match against the Argentine junior national team that he was able to appreciate my skills. Opposing us were Maradona's brother Hugo, Redondo, and Fabbri. We won 2-1, and I scored both goals.

In Rosario, Griffa offered me a place at Newell's Old Boys. I accepted, because I thought he was not serious. I was fond of football as a hobby, but I could not picture myself as a professional footballer. Besides I had still one year at school, and my parents would never have consented to my leaving. I talked the matter over with my father, it was a rather general discussion, I wasn't enthusiastic about the idea.

I was no longer thinking about that offer when Griffa telephoned me. I didn't know what to do; in my heart, I wished my father would not consent. Instead, he had told me in no uncertain terms: 'Go, if you want to, but I can't give you any money.' And he spoke quite frankly to Griffa as well: 'I'll send you Gabriel, but you must make him study.' I said nothing to Irina, especially because it was only a trial, and, I wasn't at all sure that Newell's were going to sign me on. I had no intention of parting from my girlfriend, she meant a lot to me. After my trial, though, some people from Rosario began to pester my father with telephone calls, and each time they wanted to talk to me. 'You must come, Gabriel, you'll have a good time here, you'll score a lot of goals and play on the best football grounds in Argentina.' It was difficult for me to resist. And one day we decided – my father and I – that it was worth trying.

It was at that point that the dark car appeared. It was parked in front of my gate, and I immediately noticed it didn't belong there. There was something unusual about it, and it wasn't only the colour. I understood what it was all about later. It was my destiny. Griffa had sent one of his men to fetch me, his name was Altieri. 'Pack up, we're leaving,' were his only words. It was January 1987, the weather was hot, the streets were covered in dust. I couldn't understand what was going on, and there wasn't enough time for me to think. My mother was out to buy me a pair of jeans. I spoke to Irina in uncertain terms; I told her not to worry, because I would be back in a couple of weeks at the latest. I can't remember why we left the dark car in Reconquista, maybe it was out of order. But the people in Rosario were looking forward to seeing me, so we got on a coach that left from outside my gate at two o'clock in the afternoon. We reached Rosario at ten at night – eight hours to cover about 280 miles. There were faster coaches, but this one was cheaper.

It was OK for me, but Altieri, who was not used to that uncomfortable means of transport, cursed the streets of Argentina all the trip through.

Rosario looked like a metropolis to me. From the window of that run-down coach, I could see strange faces. I wasn't happy. Altieri took me to the stadium, which was inside a park; underneath the stands were the sleeping quarters for the younger players. Altieri showed me my room: inside it, there was a bed, a mattress, as hard as the stones in the 'earthworm' football pitch, a grey locker, and that was all. Of course, we all shared the same bathroom. People who find themselves in the same plight often become close friends. This was where I met Gustavo Masat. We had both played for Reconquista before, but he came from a small village called La Garza. We haven't parted since.

Translated by Maria Alessandra Scarile. Extracted from Io Batigol Racconto Batistuta, *published by San Marco Sport Events (Montecantini Terme), edited by Alberto Polverosi, Alessandro Rialti, Alessandro Bocci and Stefano Pucci.*

the green green grass of anfield

LIZ CROLLEY

Finding a 'speck'

Before my first match at Anfield I had only ever seen Liverpool play on TV. As we only had a black and white TV at home I had only ever seen Anfield in various shades of grey. This did not prepare me for green grass. Yes, embarrassingly, all I can remember of my first match at Anfield is the bright green grass.

The only credibility I gained via not recalling anything at all about my first game was that friends assumed I was too young to remember and once this had circulated around the school a few times, I was apparently just a babe in arms when I was first led to the singing on the Kop.

Anyway, other than that the grass was green, memories of most early matches in the 1970s all merge into one. Other children's parents (usually fathers) brought a milkcrate for them to stand on but I sat on a bar. My mum stood behind me and held onto the hood of my coat. I'm told I went to the match on more than one occasion in a red and white dress, with ribbons in my hair, but I'm not too sure whether or not to believe this malicious accusation.

At this stage, knowledge and understanding of the game were irrelevant to its enjoyment. I thought players were good because I heard other people say they were good. I didn't notice that Keegan and Toshack linked well together until someone informed me that they did. I loved Steve Heighway because he was fast and because a great 'Ooh' of expectation crescendoed around the ground when he attacked down the wing. It was a long time before I cultivated a footballing mind of my own and since I was rarely asked my opinion on the technical side of the game anyway (females are only ever asked our opinions on the atmosphere or the players' kit), I was into my teens before I had grown in confidence enough to volunteer my opinion.

Amazingly I was attracted to terrace culture at least partly by its men. No, I was no lascivious girl craving the attentions of virile, magazinesque models of masculinity. Instead, I was faced with sweating, smelly, unshaven and slobbering heaving hordes of men who grabbed hold of me and clung to me when we scored. And I found they actually held a certain attraction. I learnt at a young age to exploit the opposite sex, and these strangers, who amusingly seemed to believe that little girls needed more protection than little boys, always looked after me and made sure my younger sister and I didn't fall off our bar and that we could see at least a patch of green.

Whenever we scored a goal I'd be thrown about like a rag doll (fine, I couldn't have stayed on the bar anyway) and kissed by what I could only imagine were nettles growing out of these men's faces, reeking noxiously of stale ale. Still, it was a small price to pay for being more or less guaranteed to stay on the bar all through the rest of the match and for Liverpool scoring a goal.

It was usually much easier to get an excellent view of wherever the ball wasn't than to follow the ball around the pitch because everyone else's heads, all much larger than mine, were trying to do the same thing. In this way, I became fully aware and appreciative, even as an infant, of the amount of running players did *off* the ball.

Nowadays, nostalgia for the terraces is only ever a sigh away. This is surprising for several reasons. If I try to describe what it was like standing on the Kop, even I cannot see its attraction. The swaying and pushing of smelly bodies. Whiffs of cigarette smoke in your face. Furthermore, women are far less likely to get touched up by groping men now we are seated. Personally, I suffered very rarely from such incidents. The one occasion when I felt a hand roam into a dangerously private area, I grabbed it and twisted the finger back so hard I heard it crack. I was lucky. From then on I always stood with one arm by my side in case the occurrence should be repeated.

One of the girls who started standing with me when I was in my mid-teens put up with an old man's hand between her legs for almost the whole of the second half before she managed to get close enough to me to mention it. She was thirteen at the time. Public humiliation was our only ammunition. I remember calling him a pervert, telling everyone what he was doing, but no one seemed especially interested. It wasn't until the end of the match when I met up with my sister who had drifted a good thirty yards during the game that she informed me he'd tried the same thing on with her in the first half. Two thirteen-year-old girls did not pose much of a threat to this man. Who knows how many others he had tried to manhandle in the days of the Kop.

The football family

With the exception of my dad, (a season-ticket holder at Goodison), the rest of my family were at the outset my 'football family'. I went to the match with my mum and my sister, and then with my brother. They were core members of my 'football family' for many years. I was an 'Annie Road Ender'.

My independence as a fan commenced when I began to establish my own 'football family'. This must have been around the age of thirteen when you want to make a point of being able to do everything by yourself. It was important that I was perceived by others to be able to stand on my own two feet – literally. I chose my first 'speck' in a similar position to my second and final resting place, but about thirty yards further back. This is where I met the people who were to become the closest members to me of the 'football family'. I had progressed to the Kop.

At that time, some of my (female) friends from school were flirting with the idea of going to football matches. Naively, I believed they were being educated into football culture and were showing early signs of getting hooked on Liverpool Football Club.

Much later I realised it wasn't the football they were interested in. It wasn't the Kop, but the (male) Koppites they were flirting with. I had introduced them to heaven – a heaving mass of virile young men who were laying open their emotions in such a way my friends had never seen before and, more importantly, they were not expecting in the least to be the subject of scrutiny of the lustful kind. My friends were delighted with Anfield.

Few of these friends ever returned more than a couple of times, however. This is one of the reason why I fiercely reject any (male) assumptions that female fans only go to football to manhunt. It is an accusation I will always contest. At most, a few females, like my old schoolfriends at the age of thirteen, might go for a glimpse of their pin-up stars (although there were precious few of these in the days of Rush, Beardsley, Lawrenson and Co.) but even teenage crushes are easily bored by watching their heroes jog around a park every now and then. Or they might try a football match to go on the pull, like my schoolfriends. In these cases, their early optimism is tempered rapidly by the realisation that 'the lads' aren't interested in amorous interludes at the match. They want to watch football.

Apart from these few females, the rest of us are fans, female fans, and like it or not, we can be just as loyal, just as knowledgeable and (sadly) just as obsessive about our team as male fans can be at their most extreme. We even choose to make that

Wednesday night trip to Plymouth in the middle of winter. 'My 'football family' has always treated me as just another fan. This has not always been the case, however, with everyone I've come into contact with over the years. Men make naive assumptions about women and football. Assumptions that we don't have an opinion on the football, only on players' legs. Assumptions that we don't like swearing. Assumptions that we go to football matches to look at men and must be slags. Other times, I must admit I've benefited from being female. The match against Man United away was one example.

Manchester United v Liverpool (19.10.1985)

It was my first away match since Heysel. After the tragedy I'd resolved to give up my away matches. I was disillusioned with football and had lost confidence in the security of the away-match routine. It seemed wrong to carry on after what happened as though nothing had changed. So away matches were my sacrifice. It lasted five matches. I had even refused to go to Goodison and missed one of Liverpool's most impressive victories in recent years (we were 0-3 up at half time). Man United was my first venture back.

I hadn't intended to go to this match. I had just started university in Manchester (chosen, information naively volunteered at my admissions interview, for its proximity to Liverpool to keep costs for home games down to a minimum). My intention was to make my way to the ground, greet my 'football family' briefly and leave them. But I was sucked into the pre-match atmosphere. The nerves started tingling. I wanted to see the game. I *needed* to see the game and, I believed, the team needed me there.

Only one problem. It was, of course, a sell-out. There was no chance of me getting in. I wandered around semi-aimlessly for a while, half expecting someone to jump out and offer me a ticket, genuine, at cost price, in the Liverpool end. It didn't happen. I began a half-hearted plea for 'Any spares?' No luck there either.

By 2.30 p.m. I'd worked myself up into a state of near panic. I had to get in. Somehow.

The fans in wheelchairs already had helpers. The women who served in the restaurants and executive boxes refused to give up their job for the day, even when they were offered remuneration. Ditto the stewards. There was no band to gate-crash. I was courting the idea of stooping to an all-time low. The tickets for the players' wives etc. were still awaiting collection. Reasons why I should have one of these tickets rather than one of the players' acquaintances were easy to formulate. I was a better fan, less fickle, more loyal. Mine was a *need* not just a desire; all I needed was the gall to walk into reception, claim to be Ms. X (I knew several useful female names to serve my purpose) and walk out *fait accompli*. But I couldn't do it.

Eventually, I'm ashamed to admit it, I explored my wily feminine ways. 'Wily feminine ways' is often just a euphemism for 'male stupidity'. How men can spend so much of their time with women and know so little about us is one of life's mysteries, but it comes in handy from time to time. Had I been male I would not have accessed Old Trafford that day.

I had never done anything like it before (except at the Everton v Watford FA Cup final in 1984 when I gave the man on the turnstile £5 to let me in – but that was different as I had chosen not to buy a ticket on moral grounds believing tickets should go to the fans of the clubs involved and I only went to show a Blue Nose mate of mine the route). I approached the turnstile with determination.

'One, please,' in my poshest, un-Scouse accent.

'Sorry, love, but it's all-ticket today.'

'Oh!' I feigned surprise.

'Yes love. It's a big match today. We're playing Liverpool.' In his most patronising tone, but I suppose I deserved it.

'So where can I get a ticket?' Innocence personified.

'You can't. They're all sold out.' For one horrible moment I thought it wasn't going to work.

'Oh!' I didn't need to pretend to look disappointed. This was a crucial moment in my plan. 'So I can't get in anywhere?' A pathetic figure, eyes down. My next step was to offer him the money with a, 'Can't you take my money?' bribe. But it was unnecessary. The kindly chap had taken pity on me and fallen for my charm.

'Go on in.' And the turnstile clicked. It was that easy. My only regret was that I had done it at the Stretford End.

Walsall v Liverpool (12.10.1988)

The match itself was uneventful, memorable only for frustrating incidents like when Rushie missed a relatively easy (by his standards) goal scoring opportunity which led to a friend next to me tutting and muttering, 'Shit!' under his breath. But apparently it wasn't quite under his breath. He was grabbed by both arms by our glorious boys in blue and ejected from the ground for swearing.

This was the fate of some ten of the thirteen of us who had travelled together to the West Midlands for this match. One by one they were thrown out with varying degrees of ceremony accused of that violent crime, swearing. I was left stood in the rain almost alone as all my companions were visible only in the distance among the crowd that peered over the corner of one of the stands, still able to follow the game.

At the time, it was mildly amusing. Those that remained were carefully shouting, 'Oh drat!' and chanting, 'Who the flipping heck are you?' to the police. I approached one of the officers on duty and asked what was going on. His response was well-rehearsed. They were cracking down on swearing in an attempt to encourage more women and children to come to Walsall.

I find no logic in this argument. How do people who are not there know whether or not those who are there are swearing? And what is the point in targeting the *away* end? If my friends are all ejected, and I stand on my own, do they really expect me to go back? Hardly a way to encourage anyone, especially women and children. And has anyone bothered to ask the women and children (always lumped together as one) how we feel about swearing? Does it not enter anyone's heads that women might object more to the barrage of overtly sexist, crude language that we face every week rather than to swearing, which most women do anyway? Swearing is a harmless way to express feelings. Sexist language, like racist language, tells us more about people's true attitudes while being influential in forming those of others. It is far more dangerous. Yet while campaigns to rid football of racism are high profile, sexism lurks on, unnoticed by anyone except by women. In any case, perhaps I'm complaining unjustly. On this occasion, as on many others, I was treated specially because of my sex.

Aston Villa v Liverpool (postponed, 26.12.1995)

This match was to be the 'football family's' Boxing Day out. It was a three o'clock kick-off. It had become something of an unwanted ritual for Boxing Day fixtures to be morning or noon kick-offs at Leicester or QPR, so this was something of a treat. Villa is a nice distance. Far enough to feel as though you are travelling to an away game while not being so far that you have to get up at the crack of dawn and get stiff, agitated and nervous on the coach. So instead, we got up at the crack of dawn anyway – in order to get to a pub in Birmingham when its doors opened to the public.

A handful of Villa fans strolled in, we sang a few songs with them and the usual friendly banter was exchanged, the type that nine times out of ten ends in disaster. But this time was the one out of ten when there was no trouble. That isn't to say everyone (bar myself, and possibly the ten-year-old boy who was the only child on the coach) wasn't totally bladdered. By the time news came seeping through at 1.15 p.m. that the match had been postponed because of a frozen pitch, not many people were sober enough to realise it.

So with the incentive to leave the pub removed, we stayed. The singing and banter continued and a fun time was enjoyed by all. Despite our desperate attempts to persuade the landlady and landlord to have a 'staybe' and keep the pub open after three o'clock, closing time sloped up on us and in effect our Boxing Day party was over.

We decided to have our day out anyway and to stop for something to eat on the way home. We were all starving as few people had eaten anything since breakfast. Those like myself who had boarded the coach at its first pick-up point at seven thirty outside 'The Cabbage' in Liverpool, who had stumbled out of bed around half past six and left the house without so much as a piece of toast were ravenous by now.

Before we stopped for food, priorities being what they are (and obviously people had built up quite a thirst during the five minutes we had been sat on the coach), we pulled up at an off-licence to stock up for the journey home. This was our big mistake. About a third of the coach stumbled off and tottered across the road to the off-licence. What came back was a disproportionate amount of ale for a journey that was to take a maximum of two hours. It is impossible for any of these men to go into the shop and buy two cans for the journey home, no matter how short. Their ego simply doesn't allow it.

After less than ten minutes, the familiar vision of flashing blue lights could be seen via the back window of the coach. We were pulled over by not one police car but five. Surely they weren't going to do us for taking alcohol to a football match (this was our habitual crime) when the match had been cancelled? Whatever it was, it quickly became apparent that it was serious, at least murder. Police swarmed onto the bus with their police dogs, swinging their batons. Overhead, a police helicopter hovered. The police often seem to behave in this way when they are scared or apprehensive about a situation. It's as though they aren't quite sure who has control of the situation, and they try to compensate for their lack of self-confidence by behaving themselves in a totally uncivil manner. They made my hackles rise immediately. The other occupants of the coach remained surprisingly unruffled.

'Have you lot been drinking?' quipped one alert officer.

'Is there any alcohol on the coach?' another inquired. There was alcohol everywhere. On every seat, occupying every inch of the luggage rack, in every hand, and on everyone's breath. But what was the problem? No one had acted in anything but a civil manner.

'Where did this alcohol come from?'

'From the off-licence down the road,' we replied obligingly.

'Oh, Scousers, you think you're funny, don't you?' Why does everyone outside Liverpool always accuse Scousers of thinking we are funny? I am yet to hear a Scouser say they think they have a good sense of humour. With the exception of one or two 'professional Scousers', we do nothing to perpetuate the myth.

'Have you got receipts for all this alcohol!'

The lesson to be learnt is that we should always keep receipts for absolutely everything, just in case we get stopped by the police a few miles down the road and accused of stealing it. Fortunately, the incident was being taken none-too-seriously by most people on the coach. We were having a good day out.

Half an hour passed and still no one had told us directly why we had been pulled over. It was time for the more streetwise among us to point out to these police officers that either they were arresting us or we were free to go. Legally, they could not keep us in this limbo. Their answer was unsatisfactory. We were not free to go yet – but no one was arrested, and we were still told nothing officially about why we had been stopped in the first place. Issues of legality and illegality don't seem to matter when you are a football fan.

None of the officers knew what to do. It had become apparent that we were not a bunch of yobs who were about to kick off on them. Some officers even looked rather embarrassed about the overkill. Eventually, after almost an hour, we were told we were all being arrested under suspicion of theft of alcohol from the off-licence. All forty-two of us, except the driver and the child.

Apparently, they had received a call from the owner of the off-licence who was complaining that a coachload of Scousers had come into her shop and stolen her goods. The fact that we were Scousers did not help our cause.

'Any drink you don't have receipts for will be confiscated.' A bit harsh, surely. What about my carton of Ribena I'd brought with me? Had I kept the receipt from Asda the week before? Would they let me go home and get it to prove my innocence? It was an ephemeral instant of semi-panic.

At the police station there was a handwritten notice on the door which read 'No Robbing Scousers by Order of Management'. I was outraged by the sign and mentioned it to one of the officers. 'Oh, that was there before we arrested you lot,' he said. 'Scousism' is a socially acceptable form of racism. Would they have got away with putting up a sign which read 'No Robbing Blacks by Order of Management'?

It took yonks for three officers to custodise forty people. Forms, each including a handwritten statement of events, had to be filled out for everyone. You would have thought that in the 1990s, we would have developed a system rather more advanced than that. The waiting room accommodated half a dozen people, the rest waited patiently in a queue which led out of the door into the cold December darkness outside.

It was around eight o'clock by the time I was custodised. The cells were all more than full by this stage and 'You'll Never Walk Alone' was inevitably ringing throughout the station. The form seemed straightforward enough. So why did it take half an hour to fill it in? The police officer took down my details. Name. Date of birth. Occupation. Residence. Colour of eyes. Colour of hair. Build. 'Voluptuous?' What exactly did he mean by 'voluptuous'?

'Well, you know.'

No I didn't know.

'Well . . .'

At this point the policeman began to squirm about and look uneasy.

'Don't you think that's a bit sexist?' His gaze shifted. He couldn't look me in the eye. I almost felt sorry for him.

'I didn't mean it as an insult. It's really a compliment.' That old chestnut. I explained to him that the dictionary definition of 'voluptuous' would be something like 'promising sensual gratification', and asked him how he would like it if he was described as 'well hung'. Embarrassed, he acknowledged my point. Yet I could judge from his expression that his feelings ran along the lines of, 'We've got a right one here.'

The police officer proceeded to write the statement of events, which I was, I assumed, to sign at the end. How could I tell whether or not it was accurate if I couldn't read the handwriting? I asked him to write a bit clearer as I couldn't read it. 'Oh, that doesn't matter,' he said. But when he then asked me to sign his three pages of scribble he had to go through it word for word with me. I corrected his grammar and spelling with great pedantry.

I wasn't taken to my cell until around half past eight. Inside there were three other women. The woman's cell was *en suite* – a dubious privilege as, instead of being released from the cell and taken for a walk to a nice private toilet, we had our toilet in the corner of the cell and had to use it there in front of one another. I was relieved it wasn't me who suffered the ignominy of it being *that* time of the month.

As it was, our stay in the cells was short-lived. The women were the first to be released. As I had been the last in, my visit was even shorter than everyone else's. By around midnight, it was becoming clear to the police that they really couldn't keep us there much longer without preparing forty-two portions of bangers and beans. We had eaten nothing all day.

Some saw me as fortunate because of my short stay in captivity. I see it less favourably. Last in, I had stood the longest outside in the cold. First in, I had the longest to wait on the coach outside waiting for the rest to be released in trickles, one by one. In short, I had spent just three hours in the relative warmth of the cell while some had spent seven or eight. This positive discrimination on the part of the police might be perceived as being healthy and considerate. Without knocking what was undoubtedly an honourable attempt to put us feeble females through as little suffering as possible, I merely suggest that had the brainwave been thought through properly, the conclusion might have been to leave us to sit a little longer indoors.

I later complained to the police about the nature of our arrest. The author of the letter of response gave a back-handed apology for the notice about Scousers saying that '*if*' such a notice existed, it 'would have been' inappropriate, but added that he had asked the officers on duty that day about it and they had denied all knowledge. I actually took the notice off the door and still have it. I received no reply to my follow-up letter.

The changing football experience?

By and large my experiences are similar to those of any other Liverpool fan. Undoubtedly, the football experience has changed considerably over the last two decades. We sit. We can travel to away games wearing team colours. There's (soft) toilet roll in the ground. We see the 'haves' of society around the ground more than the 'have nots'. We sing less.

I am aware of talk of the 'feminisation' of football. True, more women than before seem to occupy certain parts of certain grounds, but the atmosphere remains distinctly male (just like the House of Commons, I suppose, where despite the new influx of female MPs, it's still the male voices you hear mooing in the background). The balance of power hasn't changed.

jaap stam: without his christian name he doesn't exist

GUUS VAN HOLLAND

A man with wooden blocks for shoulders, tree trunks for legs and a head of iron. Strange that a man like that can run so fast, can turn around without falling down like a sack of coal.

These seem denigrating qualifications for the physical characteristics of Jaap Stam, a footballer valued at £10.5 million by Manchester United. But anyone who has seen him play for PSV and Holland understands that there is nothing about Jaap Stam that calls for a negative judgment. Jaap Stam is simply Jaap Stam, a footballer of one piece. Nothing more, nothing less. £10.5 million, 35 million guilders. Never has so much money been paid for a Dutch footballer. And that for a defender, a defender without the allure of Franz Beckenbauer, Gaetano Scirea, Franco Baresi, Daniel Passarella, Ronald Koeman, Frank de Boer or Paolo Maldini. Why is Manchester United so delighted with this Dutch *cheesehead*, who cannot approach the moves of Dennis Bergkamp, Ronald de Boer, Phillip Cocu and Boudewijn Zenden? Those English must be crazy.

That is how the Dutch react every time this mega-transfer is discussed. In the café in my village under the smoke of Amsterdam, they laugh themselves crooked. They scream with laughter whenever the name Jaap Stam is mentioned. They begin roaring anyway whenever the name of a PSV player is mentioned. Then they slap their thighs and begin jeering. It is, after all, an Ajax café. They all saw on television how in May, during the Dutch Cup final, Jaap Stam was turned inside out by Shota Arveladze,

Ajax's tricky Georgian. They saw how Jaap Stam with his big body was turned about and finally took revenge by kicking Arveladze on the ankle. Usually Jaap Stam doesn't let himself be tempted into acts of revenge. But for him this must have been a very unpleasant match indeed. It was, in the Rotterdam Kuip, his farewell match with PSV. To lose 5-0 – Jaap Stam could not remember ever losing so heavily. In his youth, perhaps, but not often.

Now the people in the café in my village are not in the least objective. There are no football cafés with objective football nuts. Sometimes the bar is full of orange balloons, sometimes red-and-white ones. Orange or Ajax, they don't have any other tastes. Fred Grim, the Ajax reserve keeper, is the most famous inhabitant of our village. When he drops in, the tap opens and never closes again. He was in again recently. He had brought his little daughter along, ordered an ice cream for her and a cola-rum for himself. '*Hè, Fredje!*,' the café called out, when he walked in with his eternal big smile. It was the day after Jaap Stam had scored an own goal in the semi-final of the Dutch Cup. PSV had narrowly beaten FC Twente 2-1. '*Hè, Fredje*, that Stam comes from Cambuur Leeuwarden same as you, doesn't he? Did he score that many own goals when you were there, too? What a bastard, that Jaap Stam! Is that what they're paying 35 million guilders for? Do you get it, *Fredje*?,' shouted one inside-out barfly.

Fred Grim is usually in for a joke, like most Amster-dammers. But this time he was serious. 'Listen,' said Fred Grim. 'PSV is a shit team, I wouldn't play there for any money, I'd hang myself from the crossbar if I had to stand in goal there, I'd let in every ball that came to me. But if Jaap Stam should somehow threaten to score an own goal, I would do everything to keep the ball out. He's a footballer who never leaves you in the lurch. A golden guy. It's a shame he plays for

PSV. But more than anyone else he deserves to earn golden money at Manchester United.'

It was quiet for a moment, because it is always quiet when Fred Grim says something in the café. That's how much respect there is for Edwin van der Sar's stand-in. Then one man began grumbling, and someone else too. A couple even began jeering. Fredje actually became angry. For a moment he threatened to throw his glass of coke in somebody's face. 'You leave Japie alone,' shouted Fredje. His daughter began crying quietly and dropped her ice cream. What happened next borders on the miraculous. Suddenly the whole café, all of them Ajax fans, stood up. They picked up their beer glasses and sang, 'Japie wins the World Cup, Japie wins the World Cup,' followed shortly afterwards by 'Fredje Olé, Fredje Olé.' Someone almost began singing the PSV song, but Fred Grim just managed to prevent that. Imagine if it had become known that the Ajax reserve keeper had encouraged a whole café to sing the PSV song. Old Grim would have been sacked immediately.

Anyone who walks into that café and mentions the name of a footballer who doesn't play for Ajax is jeered out of the door. It happened to me when I shouted once that Zinedine Zidane of Juventus had taught all the Ajax players a lesson in football in the Amsterdam Arena. It was true. But I was almost lynched. I still look through the windows of the café to see who is inside before I get my beer. 'That *klote* football journalist doesn't like Ajax,' I sometimes hear. And if you don't like Ajax, they think you must support PSV or Feyenoord. I don't really support any club, although I must admit that I am very attracted to Juventus, AC Milan, Real Madrid and Benfica, particularly to Brazilian footballers and even a bit to Manchester United, the club of one of the idols of my youth, George Best, the club Jaap Stam has supported all his life. But Ajax supporters won't tolerate supporters of other clubs in their bar, and certainly not of Feyenoord or PSV. Feyenoorders are their arch enemies. Nothing special, really. But if you're for PSV, you are even worse. You must be dumb, they say. It's the club for provincials, the people from Brabant with their soft 'g' and their dumb talk. A PSV-er is from the factory club of Philips. The Philips Sports Club is known in Holland (the western part of the Netherlands) as the Provincial Sports Club.

I hate Ajax supporters. I hate Amsterdammers. I hate their big mouths, their delight at themselves and their short-sightedness. It drives me mad to hear the way they talk about Amsterdam, Amsterdam as the centre of the world. The way Louis van Gaal used to scream it like a demagogue. They don't know any better. They don't know that Amsterdam is only a village with beautiful canal streets and beautiful footballers. I hate Amsterdammers because they look down on everyone who is not from Amsterdam. I am not from Amsterdam. I come from the provinces. Not from Brabant, like PSV, let that be understood, but I do have the accent and the humility of a provincial. I have something that Jaap Stam has too. Just like me, he comes from the east of the Netherlands. Where they talk in a slightly gnawing way, like farmers with chewing tobacco behind their jaws, and where they stamp a bit when they walk, like farmers on clogs.

I feel a little akin to Jaap Stam. I am even slightly jealous of him. He is the provincial who did become a professional footballer, and I didn't. Why him and not me? I even think I was better. But maybe I didn't have as much persistence as Jaap Stam, maybe I was too uneven and temperamental, not as balanced as Jaap Stam. Just like me, he played Saturday amateur football, the kind of football that people – wrongly, I think – imagine to be less skilful than Sunday amateur football because it is played chiefly in farming and fishing villages. In Holland there are two kinds of amateurs. The clubs that play on

Saturdays are mainly from communities where playing on Sundays is forbidden. These are clubs from Protestant communities and villages where people are only allowed to get into motion on Sunday to go to church and pray to God and thank Him for His blessing. Someone who does move on Sunday, let alone goes cycling or plays sport, is admonished loudly by the pastor from his pulpit. Hell and doom await him. And that is very frightening, I can tell you.

I often played in the town where Jaap Stam grew up, Kampen, in the northern middle of the land where the Yssel river flows into the Ysselmeer. A real town, with walls around it and a real city gate. Kampen has a Theological School and a Christian Academy for Journalists. The town goes to church on Sunday mornings and afternoons in large numbers and stands by the touchline at Go Ahead Kampen or DOS Kampen on Saturdays. I often played there. Good, strong teams with sturdy, unyielding footballers who never let themselves be tempted into a curse. They played hard, bonehard, ruthlessly. On the touchline the people screamed as if the Devil they feared had to be defeated. I never felt good when I had to play there. Panting defenders in my neck, heavy tackles on my ankles. And if I grew angry and shouted, 'Goddammit' from the bottom of my heart, then everyone on the touchline screamed that I was a rascal, a son of the Devil even.

Like Go Ahead Kampen, DOS Kampen were often Saturday amateur champions of Holland. Because there was always a concentration of good footballers, footballers who stayed in the town and stayed in Saturday football. They never dared make the step to Sunday football – to the pros. Earning money on Sunday by playing football was a sin for which the community of God would never forgive you. Maybe it will be different for Jaap Stam. But maybe he will be punished later, when he has grown rich from football.

Jaap Stam was born in Kampen in 1972. He grew up in a family that was Netherlands *Hervormd*. Even twenty years ago, that was less heavily religious than the followers of the *Gereformeerde* Church, for whom simply kicking a football is an offence that God will never tolerate. Jaap Stam's father was a carpenter, his mother served beer in the clubhouse of DOS Kampen, and his three elder sisters stood on the touchline to cheer on Little Japie, as they called him. Jaap has known his wife Ellis since he was sixteen. She was his first love and will probably be his last. Jaap would not dare, because Jaap is loyal as a dog to his wife. Soon they will have their first child and when Jaap has stopped playing for Manchester United they will return to Kampen, to grow old quietly and normally. Jaap already has a place in mind where he wants to live, by the river, on the beautiful Yssel. There he can sit for hours and watch his fishing line. Call it silent pleasure.

Oh, that Jaap Stam is so normal. He doesn't talk much. He doesn't have that much to say. As long as he can play football and enjoy his family, friends and acquaintances. Jaap is so nice, too. And people who are nice are not special. To be considered nice is really a bit of an insult. Someone who is nice has no charisma, is a nobody. Yet at the start of this year, Dutch footballers chose Jaap Stam as best footballer in the Dutch Premier League. Not Ronald de Boer, not Jari Litmanen, not Danny Blind, not Luc Nilis, not Nikos Machlas, not Dejan Curovic or Shota Arveladze, no, Jaap Stam.

When Jaap Stam was twenty, he took a daring step. He quit his electricians' course and signed a professional contract with FC Zwolle, a professional club in the first division that plays a town not fifteen miles from Kampen. His coach there was Theo de Jong, substitute during the World Cup final of 1974, a sober, dry footballer who never said much. A Jaap Stam type, in other words. A year later De Jong took Stam with him to Cambuur

Leeuwarden, in Friesland in the far north of the country. And two years later De Jong took Stam with him again to Willem II in Tilburg, in the south. Six months later, halfway through the 1995-96 season, PSV, which had a large number of injured players, snatched Stam away from Willem II. Stam began at right-back, but once he had moved to the centre of defence he was quickly chosen to play for Holland. No one was really surprised. He belonged in the Dutch team, as a rock in the tide, as a loyal defender behind the always attack-minded Dutchmen. It's good that Jaap Stam is around, otherwise everyone in the team would be attacking.

Jaap Stam is a normal, immovable, sober defender. He has no desire for stardom. Nor will he ever. He loathes being worshipped. He never wants to be a super-idol. He wouldn't know how to cope. He never will be a super-idol. He has something that characterises a lot of Dutch defenders. Defenders like Adri van Tiggelen, Wim Rijsbergen and Berry van Aerle, manly, loyal men from the past, so sturdy and cool. But he has more than them. He has it in him to be a leader like Ronald Koeman, another provincial, incidentally. Jaap Stam is a much better defender than Koeman, but is a much inferior attacking defender. Jaap Stam is less clever than Koeman and certainly doesn't have Koeman's shot. Jaap Stam is a mix of the British central defenders Hansen, Bruce, Pallister and Adams, but much better. He seldom loses a challenge for a header and often scores with his head from corner-kicks. Jaap Stam: the English will pronounce it Jap Stem. I can hear Alex Ferguson saying it on the BBC. *Jap Stem was outstanding.* No, I'd rather hear Jack Trunk. Stam: in Dutch the name means tree trunk. Broad and sturdy with both feet on the ground. He isn't called Stam, he's called Jaap Stam. Without his Christian name he doesn't exist.

Translated by Simon Kuper.

surly serbs and other stereotypes

SIMON INGLIS

From the outside, the Dinara Hotel in Smethwick, on the edge of Birmingham, looked pretty much like most small hotels lining main roads leading in and out of provincial cities all over Britain; extensions added here and there for extra bedrooms, reps' cars parked outside and, through a bay window overlooking the main road, the familiar reddish glow of a bar. A hotel with creaky, winding corridors, plastic shower trays and fuzzy TV reception, perhaps, but no doubt spotless. Over the years I must have driven past the Dinara dozens of times.

Four days were left of the football season. Only an hour or so remained of tepid, late spring daylight. At the bar-cum-reception, three mildly perspiring businessmen had just checked in and were enjoying their first, loosened-tie lager of the evening. But from the noticeboards on the walls I could tell that this was the right place, even if, for a hob nob with the regulars, this was palpably the wrong time. In an adjacent, empty room, stiffly posed portraits of, I assumed, Orthodox churchmen, saints, soldiers and politicians looked down on a pool table and formica-topped tables. Was the sixth-century Saint Savo up there some-where? And was that General Draza Mihailovic – the Second World War Chetnik hero executed by Tito's regime – above the mantelpiece?

Many of the 5,000 or so Serbians who live in Birmingham were among the Chetniks, or Monarchists, who fled from the Communists after the Second World War. Quite how they now viewed the ex-Communist leader turned champion of Greater Serbia, Slobodan Milosevic I wasn't entirely sure. Would his photo be here at the Dinara, or would most of the clientele still revile 'Slobo' as a former red?

That was one question I hadn't put to Savo. Before he came to the football club I support, Aston Villa, and therefore into my life, like most people who scanned the foreign pages and half-watched the nine o'clock news, I could only hazily identify names like Milosevic, Karadzic, Izetbegovic and Who-everovic as baddies or goodies, just as place names such as Banja Luka, Tuzla, Mostar – wasn't that was the one with the bridge? – and Srebrenica had become associated with images of warring neighbours, corpses, and TV crews under fire. As a student hitch-hiker I'd visited Dubrovnik long before the shelling. Stood, self-consciously, on the spot in Sarajevo where Princip fired the fatal shot in 1914. In later visits I'd read Croatian fascist graffiti at Dinamo Zagreb's stadium and met angry Kosovans in Belgrade. Enough, then, to know that a smattering of knowledge about the Balkans can get you into some almighty rows.

But enough also to be intrigued by the arrival at Villa Park of a tall, brooding and darkly handsome Bosnian Serb called Savo Milosevic. That was back in 1995, at the tail-end of the worst of the civil war and I confess, some time after I (and probably millions of others) had given up trying to understand what had made the Croats, Serbs and Muslims slaughter each other with such zeal.

Bloody Balkans, eh? Full of hot-heads and professional killers. Wasn't that the real crux of the story?

Or at least someone else's story. My own story was a far, far simpler one – or so I thought – which was why I was standing there at the Dinara Hotel, in Smethwick, on the edge of Birmingham, reminding myself once again to forget all about

Slobodan and his ilk and focus instead on the other Milosevic, Savo.

Mind, it was Savo who had started it, a few hours earlier at the training ground. All I had intended to ask him, before he left for the World Cup and a new start on the Continent, was, well Savo, how was it for you in Birmingham? Now that you're on your way after three seasons at the Villa, how should we remember you? As a petulant and wildly over-rated foreign striker who cost us innumerable points with your fluffed chances? As a gifted striker who won us some memorable games, but who never quite enjoyed the service you deserved? Or a shadowy, misunderstood Balkan youth whose rugged yet balletic brilliance was never fully appreciated in Brum?

Normally I don't make a special effort to interview Villa players just at the point that they're leaving. But then I always felt that Savo Milosevic was different. If I could feel a song coming on it might go, 'Hey, Savo, guess that none of us ever really knew you, oooh oooh . . .'

But I can't. In fact all I can say now is that you were by far the most persistently baffling, infuriating and divisive footballer I have ever seen perform in a Villa shirt.

Ask any Villa fan. Savo could be lumbering one second, his boots like flippers, heavy and ungainly, and then lithe the next, as he deftly skipped, turned and wrong-footed defenders with arrogant surges of power and lightness. Then, then, he could be magnificent.

At his most inept he was, to us, 'Misalotevic' – usually with just the goalkeeper to beat or with the opposition defence in a huddle fifty yards away, already blaming each other for the goal they thought was about to be scored.

At his best, he was 'Thrilosevic' – scorer of scintillating goals in Europe and the first of our three in the Coca-Cola Cup final at Wembley in 1996.

Until that point no Bosnian Serb had ever scored in a Wembley final. And right proud of him we felt and all, and for a long time after forgave him his little moods and outbursts. Or at least we did until last January when, to add to his most common appelation of all – Milosevic, the 'surly Serb' – he earned another tag, 'Spitalosevic'.

Villa were going down spinelessly 5-0 at Blackburn when Savo gobbed at a group of Villa fans who had been baiting him for missing a simple chance. 'Savo Milosevic should never wear a Villa shirt again,' declaimed the editor of the *Heroes and Villains* fanzine. It all got rather heated. Savo went on the transfer list, refused to play if he was only named substitute, and then a few weeks later everyone kissed and made up, for the time being. If Winston Churchill had been alive he'd have described Savo as he did the Soviet Union in 1939 – 'a riddle wrapped in a mystery inside an enigma'.

But there I go again. 'Don't mention the war,' someone told me before I went in search of Savo. Not the Second World War, not the earlier Balkan Wars and certainly not the latest one.

'So was it very difficult for you coming to a country where no one really understood the war back home?'

I hadn't planned to ask the question. It just came out like that because Savo's eyes seemed too darned soulful to talk only about football.

Savo had been twenty-one when he'd arrived at the Villa from Partizan Belgrade, our record signing of £3.5 million, in June 1995. Earlier that summer Villa's recently appointed manager Brian Little had tried to sign Les Ferdinand, Chris Armstrong or Stan Collymore (after deciding, apparently, not to bother with Dennis Bergkamp); the idea being that a tall, powerful number nine would be just the foil needed by our nimble-footed striker, Dwight Yorke, or 'the Calypso Kid' as the local press would often have him (since he comes from Trinidad and Tobago and smiles a lot). Dwight's best friend, by the by, is the West Indian batsman Brian Lara, who currently plays for Warwickshire, down the road from Villa Park.

Oh yes, quite an international sporting hub is Birmingham. Quite an international city altogether, actually. In fact, while I was standing on the pavement outside the Dinara Hotel, thinking of 'surly Serbs' and other stereotypes, and smelling the tang of curry from a nearby Balti House, barely two miles away preparations were in hand for the city to stage the Eurovision Song Contest and the G8 Summit of world leaders.

Now if both events had been held in the capital, few Londoners would have even noticed. But as seventy-eight-year-old Mavis Stone said when she sat down in a Birmingham canal-side pub for lunch and Bill Clinton pitched up at the next table, 'I nearly choked on my tuna salad ... my husband Ron was gawping so much his chilli con carne went cold.'

Now I could ask, how likely would it be for Clinton to go into a London pub and find himself next to a couple called Mavis and Ron? But I draw more comfort from the fact that amid all the supposed sophistication of Birmingham's burgeoning leisure and entertainment business, focused around the new Convention Centre and Symphony Hall, Ron and Mavis were still ordering tuna salads and chilli con carne rather than chargrilled tiger prawns with a rocket salad in balsamic vinegar dressing. And that across the road from the indoor arena where the Eurovision was taking place, it wasn't Winston Marsalis playing at Ronnie Scott's but the Spencer Davis Group. So glad they made it.

On the whole, most Brummies know that Birmingham is actually rather a pleasant place in which to live. In fact it's their little secret, and if outsiders share a different view, few Brummies give a toss. Though quietly proud of their own achievements, they also remain the hardest people in the world to impress (except if you are Bill Clinton). Unless you made those boots yourself, say Brummies, don't even think of getting too big for them. And don't imagine that they'll stay shiny for too long either.

All the same, when Savo arrived in 1995 I sensed that many Villa fans felt, like me, a teeny-weeny bit chuffed. That a player reportedly being courted by the likes of Juventus and Sampdoria should have opted for Villa suggested that perhaps we weren't so provincial after all.

On the other hand, knowing the Villa, there had to be a catch. Surely, after failing to sign all the other bigger names Savo was a last resort. Rumours spread, as they do whenever Villa buy an expensive player, that chairman Doug Ellis had signed Savo above the manager's head (always an uncomfortable image, in my view). Worse, that the decision had been based largely on the evidence of a cleverly edited video showing some of the seventy-nine goals Savo had scored during the previous three seasons in the rump of the Yugoslavian league, in which only Partizan and Red Star remained as significant forces.

It was a great story nevertheless. Ellis and Little, it transpired, had made a 'secret trip' to Belgrade in June, which in the circumstances seemed highly daring, even if the nearest fighting was miles away in Bosnia. Then when Savo arrived in Birmingham his forehead was swathed in a swashbuckling headscarf. It was only a temporary affectation, to cover a head wound he'd picked up in a recent international. But when you're a twenty-one-year-old Bosnian Serb from 'war-torn' Yugoslavia, then 'the official Aston Villa bandana', on sale at the club shop, priced £6.99, was unlikely to be far behind, was it?

Savo himself, with his broadly honed, expressive features, pearly white teeth and Valentino eyes, proved far too enigmatic for the local press to make out at first. One day he was 'stern-faced' and 'serious looking', the next 'happy and smiling'.

On one issue everyone was agreed. Savo's girlfriend Vesna, who accompanied him to a welcome photo-shoot at Villa Park, in a light pink trouser suit, white T-shirt and a bare midriff, was pronounced to be both charming and delightful. What the journalists and photographers who descended upon the couple really meant – and frequently discussed in subsequent months, nodding and winking – was that she was, no kidding, drop-dead gorgeous.

The 'lovely Vesna', it transpired, had been a top fashion model back home, but now she was ready to give it all up for her man. She had met Savo in a café, not knowing that he was a big star, twice winner of the Yugoslav Player of the Year Award, no less. And so Savo and Vesna became the Beckham and Posh Spice of Belgrade – shining lights of youth and wealth amid a crumbling city toppling under hyper-inflation and economic sanctions.

While Vesna effortlessly charmed the wide-eyed local media, Savo, it was reported, had been a modest lad back home, still living – according to one report – in a cramped flat with his parents, grandparents and two brothers. This later turned out to be untrue – maybe a stereotype editor somewhere confused Belgrade with Moscow (an easy mistake, we've all done it) – but at the time it sure helped to stoke the goodwill we naturally felt towards Savo. From besieged Belgrade to the borders of Spaghetti Junction, from Balkan obscurity to the international showcase of the Monday Night Match – you had to feel happy for him really.

And excited too. Gossip soon spread of Savo's brilliance in training. 'The things he can do with a ball . . .' gasping admirers told their mates after a trip to the training ground at Bodymoor Heath. One said he had the physique and balance of Van Basten. Another talked of a swerving free-kick that had amazed the whole squad. Savo himself promised to score twenty-five goals in his first season, adding that he'd never yet failed to reach targets in the past.

That was perhaps his first mistake. Brummies don't take readily to a boaster.

For those of us who had not made the pre-season friendlies, our first sight of Savo came on the opening day of the 1995-96 season: a glorious August afternoon at Villa Park. The previous season, under new manager Brian Little – a former darling of the terraces – Villa had just escaped relegation, and yet now they were outside favourites for the championship. Apart from Savo – muscular, watchful, bandana-less – two other expensive summer signings featured in their new line-up, Mark Draper and Gareth Southgate. Nice boys, no doubt, but English, with none of Savo's mystic promise.

The afternoon went swimmingly. Better than that. Villa were three goals up by half-time and went on to win 3-1. Savo set up one, didn't score himself, and was stretchered off before the end with a leg injury. But none of us complained. It had been a scintillating first-half display, not least because the opposition was Manchester United.

Predictably over the next few days the national media harped on tediously about United's shock start, barely mentioning Villa's new-found finesse. Meanwhile the Holte End adopted a chant for our first ever foreign number nine, based on a disco hit of the time. 'Boom boom boom,' it went catchily but rather cleverly on the off-beat, 'lemme hear you say, Savo, Savo!' More original than 'There's only one Dennis Bergkamp' at any rate.

We read how Savo was being made to feel more at home by Mark Bosnich, our Australian goalkeeper of Croatian parentage. Brushing up on his Serbo-Croat, Bozzie's embrace of the newcomer reminded us that truly, football transcends all boundaries and hatreds. And just to emphasise the point, before Christmas Villa released a video called *The Squaddies* in which Savo, Bozzy and other players cavorted around Villa Park in full battle dress. Just the sort of entertainment Savo's parents back in Bosnia would have really appreciated.

Stevo and Dragica Milosevic lived in Bijeljina, a small town a long way from the war zone, we were told when Savo first arrived. Savo never talked about it much apparently, but his father had been wounded, and an uncle and two school friends killed.

By then, the early 1990s, Savo was already living in Belgrade, where he had travelled as a fourteen-year-old schoolboy to train with Partizan, the team he'd always supported. Partizan are the club of the JNA, the Yugoslav Army, which, in the days before its more recent role as champions of Serbian nationalism, often recruited young country boys in order to train them up into loyal officers.

'So,' I asked, when finally I met up with Savo, 'was it very difficult for you coming to a country where no one really understood the war back home?'

'People here don't understand what's going on in Yugoslavia,' he replied calmly, 'and from my point of view I don't care, there's nothing I can do. People don't know a damn thing about the war and they don't want to listen to the radio or TV. It's always better to have a safe place, home, life, job. Everything's perfect here in England and I understand why people don't care and say, the Balkans, it's all stupid!'

I forget the exact wording of my response, but to answer it, Savo borrowed a sheet of paper and started to scribble a map.

'Look,' he began, 'Slovenia, Croatia, Bosnia, Serbia, Macedonia. Errr . . . Five. That is former Yugoslavia.'

It's not often a football fan gets a chance to discuss modern European politics with a player from his own club, so I decided not to mention that he'd missed Kosovo from the map.

'I'll explain to you a couple of things,' said Savo, pointing to his sketch. 'There was no Bosnia in the past. That was Serbian territory and Croatian territory. There are no Muslims in Bosnia.'

He saw my intake of breath, but I said nothing. If there are no Muslims left in Bijeljina could it be anything to do with the slaughter of dozens of them in April 1992?

'No Muslims,' he repeated. 'They are all Serbs, but we were under the Turks for 400 years from the fifteenth to the nineteenth century, and some of the people accepted the Muslim religion. The Turkish government gave them jobs and houses in Bosnia and they became Muslims.'

Well, of course, I'm just a simple football writer . . .

Savo then inked in heavily the border between Bosnia and Serbia, along the River Drina, as laid down by the UN when Bosnia was granted international recognition in 1992.

'I was born by the border,' Savo went on, pointing to Bijeljina, just on the Bosnian side of the line. 'I can't accept that border because this is Serbian land. I was born there, my dad was born there and my granddad was born there and his granddad and his granddad and so it's our land. There are some Muslims, but they were all Serbs originally. When I arrived in England I tried to explain to people but they don't understand. I tried to explain that I can't be an aggressor in my own country, in my own land.'

Well, of course, I realise there are rights and wrongs on both sides, but . . . so anyway, how had Savo adjusted to life in Birmingham? Buzzing international metropolis or what? (Lots of Muslims too, I might have added.)

'Here, as soon as a training session is finished everyone gets in their cars and they go home. In Belgrade after training there was always a few groups of players going to a café or a restaurant. We were all the time together even after we have finished our work. It was more friendly. I'm not saying it was not friendly here. Sometimes I went for lunch with Yorkie and Bozzie but not very often. In Belgrade it was like every day. I missed it, definitely. It's good for the team spirit because if you're playing with someone you need to know them, not just as a player but as a person.'

We had known for some time that Savo wanted to leave Aston Villa, even though, over the past two years he turned down offers from Perugia (who were soon relegated) and Napoli (ditto). After his salivary efforts at Blackburn, Atlético Madrid's interest cooled too. But reports would regularly filter back from Yugoslavia that he had bad-mouthed Villa, his recently arrived fellow striker Stan Collymore, and Birmingham generally in the Belgrade sporting press. Savo usually claimed to have been misquoted, but since few people in Birmingham could provide accurate translations of the Serbo-Croat text, none of us knew for certain.

For their part Villa were naturally keen to get their money back, so made sure they took up their option of an extra year on top of Savo's original two-year deal. That way they'd be more likely to get a fee for him, rather than lose him for nothing under the Bosman ruling. Or as Wimbledon manager Joe Kinnear once put it inadvertently, the Bosnian ruling.

'So what was good about Birmingham?' I asked again.

There followed a long, embarrassed pause. Finally he mentioned the birth of his son, Nikola. And the goal at Wembley.

'I mean Birmingham, as a city?'

Again he struggled to think of something. 'Watching movies?' he suggested, hoping I'd ask another question. 'Watching two movies a day, at least!'

Savo didn't reach his twenty-five-goal target in his first season at Villa. He managed only fourteen, which we all put down to the fact that he was 'adjusting to the pace of the English game'. But it was still a decent season, with Villa finishing fourth in the Premier League and winning the Coca-Cola Cup. In fact Savo and Dwight Yorke were developing into a promising partnership, with the 'Calypso Kid' scoring twenty-five that season. Savo took the knocks and drew the defenders. Dwight took advantage.

And yet, doubts had soon crept in. Savo, head down, skipping one tackle, riding the next, almost blundering his way through defences at times, though not always with the ball, would, it was true, usually give everything – the statutory 110 per cent at least – at least until something went wrong. It didn't have to be very much: a linesman's flag, an unpenalised challenge or more often than not, his own inability to convert simple chances. But once he was distracted, we all knew, that was it. The 'perpetual thunderstorm', as one writer described him, was coming our way.

Once Savo's hands went up to the heavens imploringly, as if to say, 'Dear Lord, can no one else see the injustice of my situation?' you knew that it was only a matter of time before he'd either get booked, crocked, or worse, try to beat the entire opposition by dribbling back into his own half before losing it in a scrum.

Perhaps what Savo really needed was a pal at the Villa, someone who really understood him both on and off the pitch. Ardiles had Ricky Villa at Tottenham, Van Basten had Rijkaard at Milan, Careca had Alemao at Napoli. So in August 1996 Savo got his own Serbian soul-mate at Villa Park, the £4 million Sasa Curcic. An attacking midfielder, Curcic had already played with Savo at Partizan, and impressed everyone during his previous season at Bolton Wanderers. Now at last we would see the best of Savo.

'For me this is the best place in the world,' said Curcic on his arrival in Birmingham, and that was before he'd even had a chance to sample a tuna salad by the canal.

If Savo was perplexing, his compatriot turned out to be a pain. After only a handful of patchy appearances Curcic told the press that his move to Villa had been the worst mistake of his life. The feeling was mutual. In the end, he scored one goal in only twenty-three starts over nearly two seasons, and earned his biggest headlines by having £4,000 worth of plastic surgery on his nose, when he should have been at training. Several Villa players would have allegedly performed the operation on him free of charge had they but known, but at least the new nose had the desired effect. After being turned down for a renewed work permit, the new-look Curcic suddenly found a British bride, and so was able to stay on in Blighty to join Crystal Palace's fight against relegation.

Villa lost £3 million on the deal, by which time Brian Little had resigned and Savo's own standing had gone from uncertain to untenable. The team was sliding nearer towards Crystal Palace, and on one particularly morose afternoon, Villa fans started loudly bickering among themselves . . . over Savo. The contretemps ended, bizarrely, with an elderly man being marched out of the ground after haranguing a teenager who still dared to defend the Savo camp, while the anti-Savo lobby kept up the chant, 'You're not fit to wear the shirt'. Typically, Savo then scored – one of ten he netted in thirty-two appearances that season – before being injured and limping off.

By then the relationship between Villa and their troublesome striker was all but over. His detractors never wanted to see him again. His defenders, myself included, just wanted him to close the door quietly behind him and have a wonderful career elsewhere.

In fairness Savo did admit that he was wrong to have spat at the gaggle of Villa fans who had baited him that afternoon at Blackburn. And at least he had been standing way out of their range when he expectorated. ('He'd have missed even if he had been closer,' noted one wit.)

'But I was wrong,' Savo admitted when I finally met him during his last week at the Villa, 'and I said that straight away. I am emotional. That's the way I am and I don't want to change that. I'm proud to be emotional, I want to be emotional. That's good. If you like your job, if you are doing something you like, you have to include emotion.'

And then he remembered the one other thing he had liked about Birmingham. The Dinara Hotel.

Four days were left of the football season. Only an hour or so of tepid, late spring daylight remained as I entered the bar-cum-reception, where three mildly perspiring businessmen had just checked in and were enjoying their first, loosened-tie lager of the evening.

Behind the bar a stocky, middle-aged man with rolled up shirtsleeves, grey hair and a ruddy complexion watched me taking in the scene, the portraits on the wall, the pool table and the notices pinned up about community events.

'Good evening,' I had said, cheerily. 'I'm a journalist and an Aston Villa supporter and I'm writing a story about Savo Milosevic, about his time in Birmingham. Even though I lived in Birmingham for years when I was younger I'd never realised there was such a large Serbian community here, so I was hoping to find out a bit more. Savo told me that this is a sort of social centre for the community and that he often comes here to relax.'

I probably added a few ums and ahs and tangential sub-clauses along the way, but it wouldn't have made any difference had I been word perfect. The barman turned away and shook his head. Nor would he serve me a drink.

'Residents and members only,' he intoned.

'But I'm writing a sympathetic piece,' I insisted. 'I think Savo's had a bad press.' I was going to add that the repeated portrayal of Savo as a 'surly Serb' was just lazy stereotyping.

But he got in first.

'Journalists,' he looked back at me with disdain. 'You're all the same.'

Seconds later I was back on the street, wondering what to do with the rest of my evening.

Journalists, Muslims, 'surly Serbs' and football fans, I thought to myself. To someone, somewhere, they're all stereotypes. All the same.

Four days later Savo made his final appearance at Villa Park, and found himself brooding on the subs' bench next to Stan Collymore, the tall, powerful centre forward who'd succeeded him both as Villa's record signing and as enigma-general of Villa Park. And there he remained throughout the game, his three-year spell in the Premier League ending in deflating anonymity.

The following day he went off to join his fellow members of the Yugoslav squad, preparing for the World Cup, and the next we heard, a few days after that, was that he'd finally got what he wanted, a transfer. His next port of call, Real Zaragoza of Spain.

Delighted to be leaving Aston Villa, Savo reportedly told the press, 'Birmingham was a boring place. All we ever did was stay home and watch movies.'

I wonder if Savo has ever been to Zaragoza on a wet windy night in January? Well, I have, and as they say in Birmingham, quite frankly I'd rather have a biscuit.

That, and a centre forward who'd be quite happy with a tuna salad by the canal.

the match

JOSEPH O'CONNOR

The morning of the match, Eddie Hynes had a serious case of the shakes. He swept back his straggling greasy quiff, leaned forward over his desk and continued meticulously forging the expenses docket for his training course in junior bank management at the Royal College of Banking, Peckham Rye. The sun roared in through the office window, making him feel sweaty and panicky but somehow, simultaneously, not quite alert. He unscrewed the cap of the Tipp-Ex bottle and began to apply the white fluid to the dotted line with the devout delicacy of a monk. One of those fuckers who did the Book of Kells. That's what he thought. He was in a bad mood.

Suddenly the telephone rang, making him start and fumble.

'Hynes,' he said.

'Eddie,' said his sister's voice. 'It's me.'

'Patricia,' he said. 'What do you want?'

'Charming, Eddie.'

'Sorry,' he said. 'How's Paris?'

'Fine. Are you looking forward to the match?'

'Cant watch it. Have to go to a fucking wedding with Siobhan today.'

'Ah well. Sure it's only a match.'

'That's what *she* said. Fucking Ireland versus England in the European Championships and I have to go to a fucking wedding.'

'Eddie, stop swearing and listen to me. I've a bit of news.'

He picked up his coffee. 'What's that? You and fuckface Phil finally getting engaged?'

'Yeah. Funny. Now don't get excited, Eddie. But I had this accident.'

'Oh, what? He hasn't managed to somehow impregnate you, has he?'

'No . . . Just . . . look . . . I had this accident the other night, right? I'm in the hospital.'

'What kind of accident?'

'Well . . . don't go spare now, but I got run over on Saturday night.'

'You what?'

'Run over.'

'Jesus, that's . . . Are you OK? Did you get his number?'

'It wasn't a car.'

'What was it?'

'A train,' she said.

'What?'

Her voice started to crack with tears. 'Well, I was a bit plastered you see. I'd been out with Philippe and we had a row on the way home. We were pissed and I fell over onto the train tracks. And a train came along, you see, and . . .'

'Patricia. Tell me you're pullin' me wire here.'

'Eddie,' she said, 'I'm after losing a leg.'

He spluttered a mouthful of hot coffee down his shirt. 'You WHAT?'

'I lost a leg, Eddie. They had to amputate it.'

The line crackled with static. He felt sweat soak through his forehead.

'Jesus,' he said. 'Jesus.'

'I'm so scared, Eddie,' she sobbed. 'Can you ring Dad and tell him?'

He heard himself whinny with high-pitched laughter. 'No fucking way,' he said.

'Please Eddie. He'll kill me if I do it. He'll make me come home. I couldn't face it. Go on, Eddie, will you please? Please?'

'Patricia, I . . .'

'I have to go now, Eddie. The nurse is here with my painkillers.'

'Wait . . . Patricia . . . *Wait*!'

The line went dead and began to burble. He slammed down the receiver, stood up shaking and went to the window, trying hard to concentrate. His sister had one leg. It was eleven o'clock in the morning on 12 June 1988. He was on the fourteenth floor of an office block in London. Ireland would play England this afternoon in Stuttgart. The team would probably be Bonner, Morris, Hughton, McCarthy, Moran, Whelan, Galvin, Houghton, Aldridge, Stapleton and McGrath. And his sister had just phoned from Paris to tell him that she only had one leg. He said those devastating words out loud.

'Stapleton and McGrath,' he said. Out loud.

My sister has one fucking leg, he thought, then. I got up this morning and I had cornflakes for breakfast and I read the pre-match reports in the *Independent* and the *Irish Times* and all that time my sister had one leg. It suddenly occurred to him that he didn't even know *which leg she had*. Was it the right or the left? He wondered if he could ring the hospital and ask. Which leg, please? How would you say that in French? *Quelle jambe, Monsieur le docteur, s'il vous plaît? Le droit ou le gauche?* Was that it? Would that do? Leaving Certificate French just did not cover situations like this.

He looked down into the street. Outside Fisty O'Grady's Irish Sports Bar, people were already milling around and drinking. A giant banner had been hung from an upper window, depicting a squinting malevolent leprechaun about to kick a

British Bulldog in the arse, all under the enormous green, white and orange words, GIVE IT A LASH JACK!

He came back to his desk, lit a cigarette, picked up the telephone and tried his father's line in Dublin. It was engaged. He noticed that his fingers were trembling badly. He tried again, dialling the numbers very slowly, hoping that this would somehow make a difference. Still engaged.

'I think you should probably sit down before I tell you this, Frank.'

'Why, Eddie? Nothing wrong is there?'

'Just take the weight off your feet for a minute, Dad,' he would say. 'Both of them.'

Well. On second thoughts, maybe he wouldn't put it like that.

Charing Cross Road seemed to shimmer with heat. Light poured from the pale blue sky and smells drifted out from the cafés, strong coffee, stewed vegetables, spiced beef and fried onions. A long line of Hare Krishnas shimmied around the corner of Leicester Square, banging their drums and chanting. A tall languid girl in an open white shirt, black bra and flowered-patterned flares ran across the street with a portable television in her hands. Outside the tube station, the newspaper man called out to passers-by 'Standard. Evening Standard.' The billboard at his feet proclaimed 'ENGLAND SET TO CRUSH JACK CHARLTON'S REP OF IRELAND.'

The English newspapers seemed to be incapable of referring to the Irish team without mentioning the manager. It was as though the name of the actual country had been changed legally to 'Jack Charlton's Republic of Ireland.' Maybe it should be, he thought. He wouldn't mind that being on his passport.

Suddenly he felt her arms twine around his waist from behind. 'Hi,' she said.

He turned and kissed her. She had on a bright knee-length dark green dress, a black silk jacket. He wanted to laugh out loud because she looked so lovely.

'I wore green for Ireland,' she said, 'with the day that's in it.'

He loved her accent, its soft Ulster inflections and rhythms, the music of its vowels.

She glanced at her watch. 'Are you right, so?' she said. 'We're really late, Eddie. My zip went. I'm putting on weight.'

'Yeah. Listen, Siobhan . . .'

'Maybe I'm pregnant,' she grimaced. 'Wouldn't that be great?'

'You're not pregnant,' he said.

'No,' she said. 'You drink too much. Your sperm wouldn't be strong enough. If I gave birth to anything it'd be a bottle of tequila.'

'Listen, Siobhan,' he said, 'there's something . . .'

She had stepped away from him and into the street, waving her hand. The taxi pulled up, leaking diesel fumes. The yellow light on the roof flickered out.

'Euston Road Registry Office,' she said.

Moving up Charing Cross Road, across Shaftesbury Avenue and onto Tottenham Court Road, the traffic was absolutely terrible. Telecom workers had dug up a long section of the street outside the Dominion Theatre and there was a parked fire brigade outside the entrance to the tube station. The inside of the car was stiflingly hot. It smelled of leatherette and lemon-scented air freshener.

'Siobhan, listen . . .'

She turned to him, licked her finger and ran it along his eyebrows.

'Mammy rang this morning to say Uncle Peter might be over from home. You'll like him.'

'Great. Listen, Siobhan, there was something I wanted to say to you.'

'Now Eddie, listen, try to be sociable today will you? And stay off the politics with Aisling. She's a bit of a republican, but a bride is entitled to peace on her wedding day.'

'How do you mean, a republican? Not another one of your quasi-provo friends?'

'Her dad was interned back in the fifties,' she said. 'With all my uncles and my dad.'

'Your dad was interned in the 1950s?'

'For IRA membership, yeah.'

'You never told me that.'

'Of course I did, Eddie. Sure everyone knows that.'

'You didn't, Siobhan.'

She smiled sexily, grabbed his hand and moved it between her bare knees. He turned away from her and peered out the window. Siobhan had two legs. His sister had one. His sister was a fucking monopede.

'What's up with you?' she asked him.

'Nothing.'

'Not still sulking about your bloody match are you?'

'No.'

'I don't know why you'd want to go and sit in some pub with a load of your mates and watch some stupid match when you could be with me. The sexiest woman in London.'

He said nothing.

'Eddie, come on. Please cheer up.'

He decided not to tell her about his sister and her leg. He would save it up for later. That would bloody well show her. Yes. That would teach her, if he said it later. Oh, by the way, Siobhan, I know you're having a really fabulous time with your hayseed woollybacked refugee from *Deliverance* relations here, but my sister had to have her leg off last Saturday night and I just thought you might like to know. It might come in handy if she was enjoying herself too much. It felt uncontrollable to him.

She poked his thigh. 'Seriously. Are you all right today, Eddie? Is there something on your mind?'

He shook his head.

'Football deprivation I suppose,' she said. 'Bad for your heart, eh?'

He said nothing.

'If you have one of those,' she said.

'You're hilarious, Siobhan,' he told her. 'Really. You crack me up.'

'Don't be such a dry shite,' she said. 'If you really don't want to come with me, you can get out now.'

He turned to her, doing his best to appear hurt. 'I do want to come,' he said. 'That doesn't mean I have to fucking like it, does it?'

The cab paused in the traffic. He looked out the window again. Another newspaper billboard caught his eye. ENGLAND SET TO TRIUMPH OVER CHARLTON'S ARMY.

The registrar was a beautiful Pakistani woman who couldn't seem to stop smiling. One of the kids, a boy of about ten, was dressed in a Republic of Ireland strip, with the word 'STAPLE-TON' on his back.

After the brief ceremony, everyone clapped, except for the bride's mother, who looked furious. Siobhan turned to him and whispered in his ear. 'Look at the mug on Auntie Betty. She's raging 'cos it's not a church job.'

'Because the fucking groom is English, you mean.'

She shook her head. 'It wouldn't be that. Uncle Martin would be more upset about that.'

'Do you know all these people?' he hissed.

'There's a lot of relations over from home. I didn't think so many would be over. I hope Uncle Peter comes.'

The boy in the strip wandered over towards them. Siobhan ruffled his hair.

'Don't you look handsome today, Johnny?' she said.

The kid blushed and buried his face in her thigh.

'You're my handsome little boyfriend, aren't you?' she said.

Outside the Camden Town Irish Centre the cars were double parked. A group of young black men in baggy jeans and baseball caps kicked a ball to each other. Loud raggamuffin music boomed from a ghettoblaster on the footpath.

The John F. Kennedy Memorial Function Room had been decorated with flowers and tinfoil stars, strings of green, white and orange bunting. White plastic tables and chairs had been arranged around the edge of the dark wooden dancefloor. Women in aprons were moving between the tables, polishing glasses, folding tricolour-patterned paper napkins into cones.

It was woollyback city. When he closed his eyes he could practically hear 'Dueling Banjos'.

He sipped tensely at his third pint of Guinness and looked around at the guests. You could tell which ones were Irish somehow, but he did not know exactly how. A waiter brought in a huge tray of drinks and put it down on a table. The groom's relations were sitting by themselves in the corner, looking restrained and politely uncomfortable in their hired suits.

Over in a corner, some of the men were watching a tiny television. It was showing previous Irish matches. A black and white Steve Heighway, dribbling a ball past defenders in tight shorts. Liam Brady looking shy and handsome. Johnny Giles with a big bushy perm and sideburns, looking like one of Lynryd Skynryd.

Where was it? The leg that had been cut off? Had a bit of it just been left lying there on the train tracks? Had some manky Parisian perv taken it home as a souvenir? Or had someone thought to pick it up and put it in a bag – a shopping bag, perhaps? – and bring it to the hospital? Would they be able to make her a plastic one? Or maybe a wooden one? Hadn't the guy who invented *The Muppets* or *Spitting Image* developed some shit-hot technique for making artificial legs?

He looked around the room, wishing he was somewhere else. He did not know where Siobhan was now, and he felt uneasy, already a little drunk and heavy. People started to come in from the bar. Somebody put on a record and a few of the younger guests started half-heartedly dancing. Then two old women began to waltz with each other, even though the record was a rock and roll song. They waltzed steadily, kind of martially, as though they had learned the steps out of a book.

He thought about his sister and how she would never be able to dance again. The thought struck him as appalling.

The lunch was chicken and fizzy potato salad and slices of greasy ham. When Siobhan asked the waitress where the chicken came from she said Tesco's in Neasden, and Eddie said it tasted like it had walked the whole way and then given itself up. Everyone at the table talked about the match. Siobhan embarrassed him by asking whether Charlton Athletic was named after Jackie or Bobby Charlton.

The speeches started. The best man said he was looking forward to getting a framed picture of the happy couple, 'preferably mounted', and everyone laughed dutifully. The groom stood up and thanked everybody for their help. When he mentioned the name of the bride's mother she stared down at her plate and began meaningfully forking her leftovers.

As the after-lunch drinks were being served, Eddie noticed an old man on one crutch came shuffling into the room. He had eczema scars all over his cheeks and a black patch over his right eye. A couple of the guests jumped up and ran to him as he began to limp painfully across the floor. He shook hands with one of them, kissed some of the women, then nudged one of them, pointed down at Siobhan and put his finger to his lips. He edged over to the table and tapped Siobhan on the back. She turned.

'Uncle Peter,' she cried, jumping up, 'I wasn't sure you'd be over.'

He hugged her hard, kissed her cheek and then slapped his chest, panting slightly.

His high-pitched voice was frail.

'Oh well, Jack Ryan ran me to Belfast. And I got the British Midland. I was treated in fine style.'

'Eddie,' she said, 'this is my uncle. Peter Toner.'

'I'm delighted to meet you, Eddie. We've heard all about you over at home.'

'You have?'

'Eddie's a bit of an intellectual, Uncle Peter. He was in the university in Dublin. He has brains to burn.'

The old man inclined his head and smiled. 'S'that Pet?'

'He was in the *university* in *Dublin*.'

'Oh yes and what's this you were studying, Eddie?'

'English.'

'Sorry?'

'*English literature*.'

'Novels, is it?'

'Well yeah,' said Eddie. 'Novels and poetry.'

The old man sighed. 'Funny how they call it English, all the same. When all the best practitioners are Irish. Would that be the word, Eddie? Practitioners?'

'Yes. I suppose so.'

'Yes. When the monks in Ireland were saving European civilisation, weren't the pagan English running around the forest in their pelts?' He coughed a mouthful of watery phlegm into a tissue. 'Still. Not to worry, eh?'

Siobhan took her uncle by the arm, led him to a chair and poured him a glass of wine. In the far corner of the room, surrounded by her friends, the bride's mother seemed to be crying. A woman was on her knees beside her, holding her hand and offering her tissues.

'What's wrong with the mother of sorrows over there?' said Peter Toner.

'She's upset, Uncle Peter, that Aisling didn't get married in the church.'

He shrugged, sloping some of his wine over his mouth and chin. 'That one's never happy unless she's something to be miserable about,' he said, then he pulled his tissue from his pocket and wiped his mouth.

A short, stocky old man with a moustache and a ruddy face came over to the table, carrying two pints of Guinness.

'Is it the blaggard Toner?' the man shouted. 'Would you look at the bloody get-up of it. Is the suit paid for yet, citizen?'

'That's Sean Moylan anyhow,' Peter Toner chuckled, standing up painfully and turning his body. 'I'd know that ignorant Cork prattle of him a mile off.'

The man plonked the pints down on the table and took Peter Toner in his arms. The two embraced, clapping each other on the back. 'How's the man. It's great to see you, *a Pheadar*.'

'Oh sure, I'm still trotting along anyhow.'

'Good man yourself.'

'You've met my niece Siobhan Kearney and her young man, Eddie.'

'I've not had that pleasure,' said Sean Moylan, shaking hands with them both. 'She didn't get the looks from your side anyway, Peter.'

'What's that? Speak up.'

'She's a *lovely looking girl* I'm saying, Peter.'

'Oh yes. She's the real ally daly. Tell me, is Maureen with you?'

'She's not been well since the by-pass, Peter. I had to make her stay at home today.'

'Oh that's a shame. Tell her I said hello.'

'I will of course. But you're looking fit to beat the band yourself anyway. You must be running after some woman today, is it?'

'What's that?'

'Are you looking for a *woman* or what, with the cut of you?'

Peter Toner laughed. 'Little point in that any more,' he said. 'I'm too old for all that caper. Thank God.'

'Oh I'd say you've a bit of spirit left in your auld still, what?'

'Pardon me?'

'Siobhan,' said Sean Moylan, 'I could tell you stories about this commanche here. From the old days.'

The old man turned to him. 'What's that, Sean? Speak up there?'

'I'm saying, I could tell them stories, *a Pheadar*. From the old days of struggle. *The yarns I could spin them, eh?*'

'Oh yes.'

'Yes indeed. The friends we love are by our side and the Saxon trembling fore us.'

'God,' said Peter Toner, in his trembling womanly voice, 'weren't they great days, Sean? I think of them often. And I seen on the paper they buried poor Mike Twomey there last week.'

'Yes,' said Sean Moylan. 'There's few did as much as Mike. God be good to him.'

'They're all going now, one by one. Joe Mullan, Shay Connolly, poor Mike now. And I see the family said no to the tricolour being put on the coffin.' He tutted. 'That's the kind of times we're living in now. Not like the good days.'

Sean Moylan nodded again. 'But sure, won't there be more good days. Better days than ever were. The republicans won't always be down.'

'Pardon me?'

'*Better days coming, Peter.*'

'Oh yes. Please God.'

They stood in silence while Peter Toner looked around the room.

'Tell me this,' he said. 'Is Maureen here, Sean?'

'No, Peter.'

'Where is she?'

'She's at home in Derry, Peter.'

'Is she?' He squinted and shook his head. 'That's funny. I thought I saw her just now.'

'Well,' said Sean Moylan. 'There's none of us getting any younger, Peter, isn't that right?'

'That's right.'

'Still, you crafty rogue, I never saw you look better in my life. If my nabs Charlton had you on his team, we'd run the English into the ground, what?'

'Pardon?'

'You look *great*, Peter, in the suit and everything. You're like that fella, John Travolta. Isn't he, Siobhan? *Who does be at the disco dancing.*'

'Where's Maureen today, Sean?'

Sean Moylan glanced at Siobhan and winked. 'I'll tell you what, comrade. We'll sit down now, Peter, and have an old jar and a natter, what?'

'Pardon me, Sean?'

'I'm saying we'll let these youngsters go off with themselves while you and I *talk a bit of auld treason, what*?'

She led him across to the middle of the dancefloor, put her hands on his waist and leaned her forehead on his shoulder. The room was very hot now, and it seemed emptied out of air. She looked up into his eyes and moved closer to him. He could feel the softness of her body through her dress.

'He's a bit gaga today,' she said. 'I'm embarrassed.'

'Don't be.'

She smiled. 'You look lovely today, Eddie.'

'So do you.'

They circled slowly in each other's arms, while the disc jockey played a slow song. 'Last night was lovely, wasn't it?' she said.

'We should have used a condom,' he said.

She looked up at him. 'I'm mad about you, Eddie.'

He tried to laugh. 'Don't say that.'

'What's on your mind today, Eddie? Are you pissed off with me or something?'

He said nothing.

'Look, they'll have the stupid match on out in the bar. All the lads here'll be slipping in. I don't mind if you go with them.'

'It isn't the match.'

'What then?'

He sighed and looked around the room. There wasn't really an easy way to put it.

'Well,' he said, 'my sister had an accident in Paris last week. She had to have her leg amputated.'

She stepped back from him, a look of disbelief on her face. 'Fuck off,' she said.

'No, really. She rang me earlier about it.'

'Jesus, Eddie. You're not serious, are you?'

'No. I am.'

Her mouth was open wide and her eyes looked frightened. 'My God almighty . . . Jesus, Eddie, that's . . . oh my God . . . did you not say you'd go over to her?'

He slid his hands into his pockets, feeling awkward. 'I didn't think. She asked me to ring up my father and tell him.'

She looked into his face. 'Oh Jesus, Eddie. The poor dote. Fuck.'

'Yeah,' he said. 'Fuck is right.'

The disc jockey put on 'Danny Boy'. Over at the table, Peter Toner and his friend Sean Moylan seemed to be watching them.

In the lobby, his father's phone was still engaged. He went into the bar and had a quick drink by himself. The room was beginning to fill up already: a semi-circle of people had formed around the television set. Eamon Dunphy was on the screen, saying that Ireland had only ever beaten England once before. While he continued to talk, excitedly and passionately, they cut to a shot of the stadium in Stuttgart. A uniformed brass band was marching in formation up and down the beautiful lime-green pitch, but the tune could not be heard because the Irish fans were already singing. 'You'll Never Beat The Irish. You'll Never Beat The Irish.' There were close-ups of some of the Irish banners. Sallynoggin On Tour. Paul McGrath – The Black Pearl. Davy Keogh Says Hello.

He asked for a double whiskey.

'Irish or Scotch?' the barman asked him.

'Surprise me,' said Eddie.

When he came back into the ballroom, she was sitting in a corner with Peter Toner and Sean Moylan. All three of them seemed to be very drunk now: she was laughing very loudly and holding her hand up to her mouth. When he sat down beside her, he felt that the conversation had been terminated because of his presence.

The plastic chairs had been arranged in a wide, untidy circle around the tables, which had been cleared of dishes and glasses. A few hairy young men had guitars and fiddles, one had a bodhran. They all looked to Eddie like the image of Jesus on the Shroud of Turin. People were arguing about who was going to start the singing.

'Any luck?' Siobhan said, peering up at him.

Eddie shook his head and told her his father's line was still engaged. He sat down and took a sip of her drink.

'Get up there Martin Thornton and sing us a song,' shouted Sean Moylan, to the bride's father.

'I will not,' the bride's father replied, shaking his head. 'I've no voice on me these days.'

' "The Men Behind The Wire",' someone shouted.

' "The Boys Of The Old Brigade",' another called. But the bride's father shook his head and took another sip of his drink.

'Well someone better sing,' a male voice shouted, 'because there's a match on soon that I want to watch!' Everyone laughed.

'Martin Thornton, get up and sing,' shouted Sean Moylan. People cheered and banged their spoons against their glasses.

'Jesus, all right, all right,' the bride's father sighed, 'I'll give you a quick few verses.'

He stood up to a chorus of jeers and whistles. Someone handed him a microphone. He pulled up the sleeve of his jacket and made a great show of looking at his watch.

'Well, Ireland do battle with England in a few minutes,' he said, and he grinned. 'And God knows, it's not the first time in history that happened.'

'Nor the last either,' someone shouted down the back. He smiled and nodded.

'Yes, today is a happy day. In a short while, there's a match going on between Ireland and England. And I suppose, when you think about it, with Aisling and Steve, that's another match between Ireland and England.' People laughed and clapped. 'I think I know who's going to win both of them,' he said, to more laughter.

His face took on a serious expression. 'But I want to take a moment today to think of absent friends. Absent comrades too, I'm not ashamed to say it. Brave men I thought would be here today at my only daughter's wedding. But who won't be. You know why and I know why. No need to dwell on it. They gave their all for their country and were happy to give it. Sometimes Aisling here, she'll say to me, Daddy, forgive and forget. And the young people now, they think that's the way forward. Maybe they're right and maybe they're wrong. All I know is, I might forgive one day, when there's justice at last in my country. But I don't think I'll ever forget.'

People shifted in their seats and looked embarrassed. Seeming to sense this, the bride's father leaned back on his heels and cracked his knuckles, gently parodying his own pomposity.

'Anyhows, I think you can all imagine what Betty and myself said when her ladyship here arrived in home one fine May morning and announced she was marrying an English lad.' People laughed nervously. 'Well, of course,' he went on, deadpan, 'we were thrilled skinny.' People laughed louder. 'Personally,' he grinned, 'I think it's Ireland's revenge for eight hundred years of colonial oppression and I therefore give it my blessing.' There was a great roar of laughter and a round of applause. Even the groom's family were clapping. Eddie noticed.

'Seriously,' he said, 'I must say, Steve seems a nice down-to-earth lad. And as for him being English, well, I think of the words of my late noble lord, the Duke of Wellington, who was once asked if it was true that he was born in Ireland. Yes indeed, he replied, but just because you were born in a stable, that does not make you a horse.'

'Ah shut up and sing, will you,' someone shouted.

'A rebel song,' another yelled.

'I was thinking earlier about what I might sing today,' he said, 'with the match being on, and something occurred to me. And I hope our English friends won't be embarrassed, if I tell you that when those lads in green go out on that field in a short time, there's another field I'll be thinking of, closer to home.'

Silence came down over the room. 'What's this is the way it goes?' he said, staring up at the ceiling. He closed his eyes then, and started to sing very slowly, in a faltering baritone voice.

> *What did I have,*
> *Cried the proud old woman*
> *What did I have*
> *This proud old woman did say.*
> *I had four green fields*
> *And each of them a jewel*
> *Till strangers came*
> *And tried to take them from me*

One of the young hairy men started to strum his guitar, trying to gauge the key. Some of the others turned to him, scowling and shaking their heads, and he put his guitar on his knees, lit a cigarette and began to listen.

> *But my fine strong sons*
> *They fought to save my jewel*
> *The fought and they died*
> *And that was my grief, she said*

'Lovely, lovely,' whispered some of the guests as he reached the end of the verse. Siobhan put her fingers in her mouth and whistled. Over in the corner, the groom's family began to look distinctly uncomfortable.

> *Long time ago*
> *Wept the proud old woman*
> *Long time ago*
> *This proud old woman did say*

He leaned forward and splayed his fingers on the table, leaning his weight on it, sucking in a deep breath.

> *There was war and death*
> *Plundering and pillage*
> *My children left to die*
> *By mountain, valley and stream*
> *And their wailing cries*
> *They shook the very heavens*
> *And my four green fields*

He paused and raised his hands, palms upwards in the air, and some of the people joined in the song with him, singing loudly, their voices soaring, seeming to fill the room.

> *Ran red with their blood, said she.*

The bride's father stopped. He laughed nervously. He seemed to have forgotten the words. He looked down at his wife. She whispered something to him, but he did not seem to hear what she was saying. He began to sing the next verse, then stopped again. He blushed, rubbing his lips with the back of his wrist. His wife stood up slowly and took him by the hand. She looked into his eyes, smiling at him, as she started to sing. He nodded as they sang together now, her voice very high, and quivering on the grace notes.

> *Long time ago*
> *Says the proud old woman*
> *Long time ago*
> *The proud old woman does say*
> *I had four green fields*
> *And one is still on bondage*

In stranger's hands.
They tried to take it from me.
But my sons had sons
As brave as were their fathers
And my fourth green field
Will bloom once again, said she.

He turned and threw his arms around his wife, kissing her hair, burying his face in her neck. She put her hands on his head, and then the bride jumped up and ran to her parents, hugging them both. Her father's face was blood-red now, tears streaming from his eyes as he sat back down. Cheers and applause filled the room. He stood up again, trembling with emotion.

'Long Live The Republican Army!' he shouted, to loud shouts and whistles.

Eddie felt Siobhan's eyes on him. 'It's a great song,' she said. 'Isn't it? It's awfully sad.'

He felt the drink pulse through his veins and the muscles tighten in his throat. 'It's a load of fucking shite,' he said. 'Four green fields, my hole.'

Her face purpled and she tried to smile. 'Don't say that, Eddie. People have strong feelings, you know.'

'If they've such strong feelings what are half of them doing living over here then? If it's so awful why don't they fuck off back to the bog they came from.' In the corner of his eye he could see that Sean Moylan was looking at him now.

'It's only a song,' she said. 'What harm is there in a song?'

'It's bollocks,' he said. 'That's what it is.'

She looked at him, her lips trembling. Then she turned to her uncle.

'Do you hear this terrible West-Brit, Peter?'

The old man turned, his one eye bleary. 'What's he saying, love?'

'Leave it, Siobhan,' Eddie sighed.

'He's saying it's all shite, Peter, about the four green fields. That's what they all think down in Dublin. All too busy being cool to give a damn about anything else.'

Peter Toner said nothing. He looked around himself like a man who had just woken up in a strange room.

'These fucking so-called Dublin wet-liberals,' she snapped. 'They'd hand the whole country back to the Brits in the morning. That's what they really want.'

'They don't, Siobhan,' Eddie said. 'They want peace.'

Peter Toner smiled, a thin rictus of frothy saliva moistening his chin. He raised his finger and wagged it from side to side. 'Ireland and England should never be in bed together, son. No peace down that road.'

'What the fuck are you on about? They are in bed together.'

'Pardon me?'

'And what good ever came of it, Eddie?' said Sean Moylan. 'Can you answer me that? In all fairness.'

'Ah, would you go back to sleep,' Eddie snapped.

Siobhan stood up, shaking with rage. 'How dare you? Don't you fucking dare speak to him like that. You little Glenageary fucker.'

Sean Moylan laughed as he reached out and took her by the hand. She sat back down, folded her arms and looked away.

'Maybe we'll leave the politics for another day, Eddie,' he said.

Eddie scoffed. 'Don't call it politics, man. Shooting people in the back of the head. Smashing their kneecaps with concrete blocks.'

The smile froze on Sean Moylan's face. 'Hold on now, buck,' he said. 'Nobody's saying mistakes weren't made. That happens in any war situation.'

'Mistakes, man? What about Enniskillen? You think blowing

up old-age pensioners for a united Ireland is a good idea, do you?'

'It's not for me to say what military operations should be. That's for others to say.'

'Listen, go and blow it out your arse, man. All right?'

'That's lovely talk now, from an educated person,' Sean Moylan said. 'The young people today, they haven't a notion of what had to be done, do they, Peter?'

'Pardon?', said Peter Toner.

'No,' Eddie said. 'They do. It's just that they don't care any more.'

'What's that?'

'They don't give a flying fuck. Ireland versus England. To me, man, that's a fucking football match and that's all it is.'

Peter Toner looked up at Eddie and tried to smile, his head quivering, his one eye half closed. 'Maybe that's what we fought for,' he said. 'So you'd have the right not to have to care. If you didn't want to. To sit in a pub and watch a football match without a care in the world. Ever think of it that way?'

Eddie drained his drink. 'No,' he said. 'I didn't.'

'You fucking West-Brit,' Siobhan snapped.

He put his glass down, stood up and started to walk towards the door, bumping into the groom, who was hopelessly drunk now and staggering around in an embrace with his best man, crying bitterly and telling him how much he loved him. Halfway across the empty dancefloor she caught up with him and grabbed his arm.

'If you walk out that door you can fuck away off,' she said. 'I don't ever want to see you again.'

'Oh dear,' he said. 'I'm scared now.'

She turned away from him suddenly sobbing, bowed her head and wiped her eyes. He reached out and touched her face but she slapped his hand away. 'You had to spoil everything,' she wept. 'You just had to.'

'Oh thanks. Fucking thanks a bunch. *What about my sister's leg?* Like, I'm really sorry here, honey, but I've got more on my mind than you and your four green fucking fields, you know?'

Tears were spilling down her face. 'If it wasn't that it'd be something else. You always have to take the good out of everything. Just get out and leave me alone.'

His father's phone was still engaged, so he went into the bar to get a drink.

The room was packed. The match had just started. One young man was wearing a green afro wig. A cloud of purplish cigarette smoke had formed under the fluorescent lights.

The commentator's voice buzzed, as he named the players in a speculative English move. 'Stevens . . . To Sansom . . . To Peter Beardsley . . . To the mighty John Barnes of Liverpool.' People were sitting around the room in groups, some of them wearing green shirts or scarves. 'Beardsley to Wright . . . To Robson . . . England advance . . . But it's a free kick to Ireland . . . Free kick to Ireland in the sixth minute . . . A little . . . debate about it from Stevens. But Referee Mr Kirschen very definite there.'

'How's it going?' Eddie asked the barman.

The barman shook his head dolefully. 'They're all over us like a fuckin' rash,' he said. 'Runnin' us ragged.' He filled the glass and placed the pint on the counter.

'On the house, mate,' he said. 'You look like you need it.'

And then a deafening roar exploded through the bar. It was as though a bomb had gone off. People jumped to their feet, wildly punching the air and screaming. A table overturned, sending glasses and ashtrays rocketing into the air. There were wild, hysterical whoops. Teenage girls dressed in green shirts ran into the bar from the corridor. A fat man Eddie didn't know grabbed him and kissed him. He pushed his way through the room and towards the television. He was dimly aware of the urgent sound of the commentator's voice, but the noise of cheering in the bar was too loud to make out what he was saying.

On the screen, the stadium looked like a sea of fluttering green, white and orange flags. The camera seemed to pan along the whole length of one of the stands. Then it cut to a scrum of green-shirted players hugging each other. Players were running and diving into the pile of bodies, followed by substitutes, still in their tracksuits. A linesman ran on to the pitch and bawled at the players. Peter Shilton picked the ball from the back of his net and swung a boot desultorily at the goalpost. Ray Houghton broke from the scrum and tottered like a man drunk with joy to the touchline, where he stood with his eyes closed, his arms held out wide towards the ecstatic crowd. He jabbed at the air with his pointing fingers. The shot showed the back of his body, and the swaying forest of green in front of him. He raised the hem of his shirt to his lips and kissed it. Packie Bonner was down on his hunkers, staring at the grass, shaking his large head from side to side. He closed his eyes and made the sign of the cross. Jack Charlton's face looked like it was carved out of granite. There was a long, lingering close-up of his haughty profile. He looked absolutely dazed. He turned around to look at the crowd. Someone in the dug-out nudged him. He turned slowly towards the camera, and half-smiled, and casually shrugged. People in the bar screamed with joy.

'*Goarn, Jack, yeh fuckin' man yeh.*'

A close-up of the scoreboard now filled the screen. REPUBLIC OF IRELAND: 1 ENGLAND: 0.

'*Yessssssssssssssss.*'

And then the action replay began. Kevin Moran's free kick drifted down near the touchline. Stevens and Wright seemed confused. Sansom sliced at the ball, sending it skywards. It seemed to fall so slowly to John Aldridge, who nodded it to

Houghton, who headed powerfully past the flailing keeper and into the net. The crowd in the bar roared with cheers once again, as though it was the first time they had seen it.

Eddie could hear applause and cheering from all over the building now, from below and above, from outside in the street. In a window across the street a middle-aged woman was frantically waving a tricolour flag. The bride's father was standing in the doorway with the young strip-wearing boy from the registry office in his arms.

A heavy man with damp broken-veined eyes grabbed him by the lapels and roared into his face. 'That'll fucking teach them. That'll teach the cunts, won't it? Won't it? *Teach the fuckin' English cunts a lesson for themselves now.*'

Eddie had the strange and irrational feeling that if he pointed out that Jack Charlton was English, the man might actually headbutt him.

It was half an hour later when he finally got through to his father.

'My Jesus, Eddie,' his father said. 'That's awful news.'

'Yeah, look, Dad, don't you think you should go over or something? Do Ryanair fly to Paris?'

'Well . . . I'm a bit busy just now, Eddie.'

'Busy?'

'Well, yeah. I'm watching the match.'

'You're what?'

'I'm watching the match here with Uncle Joe and George from the office. Mighty goal, wasn't it? Do you think we can hang on till the end?'

'Jesus Christ Almighty, Frank, I'm saying your only daughter has just lost a fucking leg, man.'

'Well I know, but – *oh Jesus – oh fuck! – oh Jesus Christ!!*'

'What?'

'My God, son. Packie's just pulled off this magnificent save. I've never seen anything like it in my life!! Fuck me, this is a game and a half, isn't it, son?'

'There's one or two factors kind of interfering with my enjoyment of it, Dad.'

'Well obviously. I mean, Lineker's a bit off form. But still.'

There was silence for a moment, and then his father started to snuffle with guilty laughter.

'I'm not seeing the humour of the situation here, Frank.'

His father suddenly howled with mirth. 'Sure Patricia's as fit as you or me,' he chuckled. 'One leg my arse. Sorry, Eddie, son. I was in on the caper all along. The two girls hatched it between them. They wanted to play a bit of a joke on you.'

'What?'

'I thought you'd cop it in thirty seconds flat, Eddie. Otherwise I'd never have gone along with it.'

'What,' Frank?'

'Yes. Siobhan and Patricia cooked it up between them. I thought you'd see through it straight away. Did you not know they were winding you up, no?'

He paused, his heart thundering. Somewhere above him he could hear people singing. *'Who Put The Ball In The English Net? Hough-Ton, Hough-Ton.'*

'Well, yeah, Frank. Obviously. I mean, Christ, what do you think I am here?'

'One Packie Bonner. There's only one Packie Bonner.'

'Ooh-ah, Paul McGrath, say ooh-ah Paul McGrath.'

He put the phone down. Siobhan was standing in the lobby looking at him and laughing.

'You fucking bitch,' he said.

'I know,' she said. 'I'm sorry.'

'No,' he said. 'The Nazis were sorry. You fucking . . . unbelievable . . .'

'I didn't think you'd get so upset. I thought you'd cop that it was only a game.'

He sat slowly down on the stairs and put his fingers to his boiling face.

'I can't believe you did this, Siobhan.'

'Come back inside for a bop,' she said, taking his hand.

He pulled away from her.

'Fuck off, Siobhan. I am never in my life going to speak to you again.'

'Come on, Eddie. Don't be like that.'

He held up his middle finger. 'Swivel on it,' he said.

Her face took on an angry expression again. 'I wouldn't waste my time, you lousy West-Brit wanker.'

By the time he got back inside she had her shoes off and was dancing with the bride and groom, holding hands with them, jumping up and down to the music.

In the back of the minicab she held his hand. They sped through the empty streets of the city, both of them completely drunk, and very tired.

Westminster Bridge had been closed off by the police, and a long line of cars and lorries had formed. Plain-clothes policemen stood on the pavement with machine-guns in their hands, while soldiers searched the boots of cars. The Big Ben clock said it was half past two.

The driver cursed under his breath, turned out of the lane and sped back down the street.

'Do you think we'll ever get married?' Siobhan said.

'Urgh, God,' Eddie groaned. 'I think I'm going to be sick again.'

'Patricia only has one leg,' he giggled.

'She's legless,' Siobhan laughed.

'You're one fuckin' wagon, you are.'

'I'm not,' she said. 'I'm nice really.'

He rolled down the window and cool air flooded the car. 'So Uncle Peter's never going to speak to me again,' he said. 'Probably gonna have me kneecapped.'

'He told me he thought you were great.'

'Oh yeah, I'm sure he did.'

'He's dying, Eddie,' she said, quietly. 'He's riddled with cancer. He'll be gone in a few months.'

The driver started to hum along with the radio.

'Gone by Christmas, they reckon.'

'I'm sorry, Siobhan.'

She reached out and took his hand between hers. 'There's something about a wedding though, eh?'

'Mmmmyeah,' he sighed. 'I'm gonna heave up my ring any minute.'

Outside on the street, a group of dejected-looking English fans were trudging along. Union Jacks wrapped around their slumped shoulders.

'So did Aisling enjoy her wedding day?'

'Yeah. She told me something strange though. When she went home early this morning to collect a few things, her da had moved out of his own room and into her old one. She went in, and there he was, asleep. And it's only a little single bed, you know. And all of his stuff had been moved in, and her mother was still in the other room. Aisling said he looked like a tiny baby. He had his thumb in his mouth, you know the way babies do. And then he woke up and saw her standing there with her suitcase. And he started to cry. And he told her he loved her.'

'Really?'

She nodded. 'It was the first time he ever told her that. Imagine.'

As they turned onto Lancaster Place and onto the approach road for the bridge, the blue flashing light of a police car appeared in the rear-view mirror.

'I feel sick, Siobhan,' he said.

She did not seem to be listening to him. She was staring ahead at the street, softly gnawing her lip. Then she turned to him and smiled and touched the side of his face. 'I love you so much,' she said.

He gazed at her, as the tears began to form in his eyes. 'Yeah. Well, I love you too.'

She nodded. 'Try not to get so excited about it.'

'Sorry. I get a bit scared, that's all.'

She put her hand on his thigh. 'We'll be OK,' she said, gently. 'I wouldn't ever hurt you, Eddie.'

The police car pulled out into the middle of the road and started to overtake. The officer in the driver's seat stared in through the window at Eddie with a frown on his thin pale face. He turned to the driver and seemed to say something, then turned back to glare at Eddie again. He motioned for the driver to stop.

The night was surprisingly cold. A fresh wind whipped up from the river. Gulls whirled around in the air, screaming and crying. Somewhere in the middle distance a burglar alarm was wailing. Thunder rumbled. Down towards the east, the dome of Saint Paul's towered over the city, and the blue lights of the NatWest tower glimmered in the mist.

By the time they had finished searching the car, Siobhan was fast asleep in his arms on the edge of the pavement.

'Sorry about all this,' the policeman said. 'We had a bomb-scare earlier.'

'Yeah,' Eddie said.

'You watch the match?' the policeman said.

'No,' said Eddie.

'You know who won?' said the policeman.

'Yeah,' Eddie said.

'Only a game though, eh?'

'Yeah. Only a game.'

He pointed his torch at him. 'Bloody get you next time though.'

'It's a date,' Eddie said.

Siobhan stirred. He held her tightly and kissed the corner of her mouth. She murmured and twined her fingers through his. And she looked so beautiful now, and so happy too, that for one long moment he did not want to wake her up and take her home. But the taxi driver said he was in a hurry, and anyway, it was a little too late for love.

a walk on the beach

A friend of mine tells me the following story. He and his wife – a complete bitch – are walking on the beach, they've had a row, really their relationship is at breaking-point again, and what happens . . .

Wait, I think I should start this story differently.

It was 17 October 1994, a Monday. It was a screwed-up day because it just wouldn't become day. So grey and rainy that if you had a gift for it you could easily become depressed.

No, before I continue with my account of this day, first the following:

When Ed de Goey was signed for Chelsea by Ruud Gullit more than a year ago, he didn't shake hands with Feyenoord's goalkeeper coach Pim Doesburg. That made the newspaper in Holland. No goodbye, no thank you, nothing, and to think that they have known each other for twenty years.

Pim Doesburg who defended Holland's goal eight times is the red thread in the career of Ed de Goey. Doesburg discovered the tall, stick-thin De Goey at the age of twelve at a little amateur club called Olympia Gouda. At the start of every football season De Goey would take the train to Rotterdam. In the Noordmolenstraat, where Doesburg ran a sports shop, De Goey would buy his keeping gloves. Doesburg – of whom it has been written that he is so mean that he barks in his garden at night to save money on a watchdog – even gave him ten per cent off. A couple of years later Doesburg tipped the oldest professional club in Holland, Sparta, which signed the young talent.

When Ed de Goey was nineteen he made his debut in Sparta's first team; Doesburg was his goalkeeping coach. In 1989 De Goey left for Feyenoord; Doesburg became his goalkeeping coach there. In 1992 De Goey made his debut for Holland; Doesburg became his goalkeeping coach.

So OK, it was 17 October 1994, a Monday. A screwed-up day because it just wouldn't become day. So grey and rainy that if you had a gift for it you could easily become depressed, but I have a strong impression that I have written that before. What made that 17 October worthwhile was the keepers training in a far corner of the Feyenoord complex; Pim Doesburg versus Ed de Goey.

The day after a match De Goey is never that keen on exerting himself. The fanatical, nervous Doesburg is, he always wants to give it everything. Doesburg won't tolerate headaches, excuses, moaning or laziness.

I stood behind the goal and registered.

'You drive me crazy, De Goey,' said Doesburg. 'Do you know that? Completely barmy you make me. I give you everything. EVERYTHING! Everything I goddamn have. I give you more than my wife. I have nothing left for my wife and children when I get home. I am empty. Because I have given everything to you. Do you understand that? You do fuck all. Nothing at all. I'll be home soon and then I'll be finished. Empty. No energy. And what for? What for, De Goey? In the name of heaven, what for? What's the point of this? Tell me. What's the point? I ask myself all the time.'

'Lay off, Pim, I know the story already.'

'Yeah, yeah. You don't give a shit. Course. You just go your own way. You know what's good for you, of course.'

'Lay off, Pim, it's getting annoying.'

'No, I won't goddam stop. This way you'll land in the shit. But who cares, lad? You've already achieved everything in your career, haven't you? Let's go and have a cup of tea in the canteen, lad, so that we can recover a little.'

'Good idea, Pim.'

'Your lameness drives me crazy, De Goey. Of course you think you've already made it. You tall piece of misery. But you're nowhere. You're making too little of your career. I kept going until I was forty. You'll be burned out at thirty. Because you think things are fine as they are.'

'Stop whingeing, man. Act normally. I train myself crazy.'

'That's the worst thing. You really do think that, don't you? How is it possible? You should see a video of this session. Then you'd see that it's rubbish. Rub-bish. Sir played football yesterday and is a little tired and doesn't want to wear himself out. Fuck it. He doesn't even know that he's wrong, that he's throwing away his chances.'

'I wouldn't have thought it's as serious as that.'

'You're as stubborn as you're tall, but you'll find out soon enough.'

'What a whinger you are, disgusting.'

(End of dialogue.)

When Doesburg walks off the field ten minutes later he says to me: 'Oh, you think this is funny. Well I don't. This makes me completely sick. You think I'm messing about. Are you crazy? The mentality of that guy makes me sick. What I said, I meant every word. That's what's so sad.'

De Goey later: 'I hate that man, you know. He drives me crazy. He really is mad. His constant whingeing makes me sick. Sometimes I just can't take it anymore. There are days enough that I don't feel like it, but today I really trained hard.

Love-hate? It's more hate than love. He just thinks I'm lazy, always. It's never enough.'

It went on like that every day. They genuinely believed that they weren't playing a game with each other, that the jeering was all meant seriously. Sometimes it was even more extreme, sometimes a bit less. The sparring and cattiness, culminating in hate, mutual hate – or at least that is what they thought, they thought that every day, that they hated each other from the heart – the daily sparring and cattiness were a ritual to which Doesburg was terrifically attached, which he couldn't do without, while De Goey didn't care for it. Even then I didn't believe that De Goey loved Doesburg, just as I was sure that the opposite was true. Doesburg could love the stylish goalkeeper with all his soul. Sometimes he almost salivated; at technical and tactical perfection, when De Goey danced on his front feet, launched himself to float, brought off a good or a miraculous save, and landed soundlessly on the ground. Then he suddenly saw the similarity with Van Beveren, the best Dutch keeper of all time, then Doesburg got gooseflesh, then he complimented De Goey. 'Goddammit, class, Edje! Class, lad!'

At Feyenoord Ed de Goey was sometimes teased by his teammates, who knew that he had the highest fat percentage in the squad. After practice in the changing room they told him that he was beginning to get breasts, they asked him if he had a C-cup or a D-cup, they called him Junior because of his tummy, after the pregnant Arnold Schwarzenegger in the film of the same name. Remarks in a changing room full of footballers. The impressive thing about De Goey is that the teasing did not reach him; he didn't hear it, and if he happened to catch something, he made sure it wasn't locked up in the cellar of his mind, he let it blow away.

This drove Pim Doesburg crazy. Hoarse voice. 'Look, that's what I mean about Ed. He just lets it all happen to him, he accepts it all. Nice and easy. Let them talk, he thinks . . . It wouldn't have happened to me in the changing room. Straight away I gave them what for. You have to command respect. Ed is much too easy about a lot of things. Completely wrong!'

Even then, incidentally, Doesburg thought his pupil was too fat. 'If Ed himself says two kilogrammes, I'd better stick to four. Of course he is too fat. Doesn't he have a mirror at home? I understand it, too. He's just in a very different situation now. He's married, has a son, and Ed likes sitting at home anyway. Then it's, "Ed, a piece of cake?", "Ed, an eclair?" It doesn't matter, as long as it flies off at practice. I have to chase him up, because he's easily pleased with himself.'

Without boasting – Ed de Goey is a modest man – De Goey says that he has never known fear of failure. Not in junior football, not in his first game for Sparta, not in his first game for Feyenoord, not in his debut for the Dutch team, not for the final of the European Cup-Winners' Cup on 13 May 1998. If Pim Doesburg admires him for anything then it's for his calm which is almost transcendental. De Goey is simply never afraid or tense. He is frightened only of one thing: losing his wife or child.

In 1995 De Goey faced a difficult choice, or at least that's what I thought. The birth of his child and the away match against Real Zaragoza were planned for the same day. Long in advance he let it be known that he would let the quarter-final of the European Cup-Winners' Cup go. Clasping a baby to his chest: everything else was subordinate to that. Pim Doesburg – and many other ex-footballers – did not agree. Doesburg's first child was expected on the day of Sparta–Ajax, 12 February 1965. Because Pim junior was born a week earlier, on a Sunday when Sparta did not have to play, Doesburg could be present at the birth, but he swears until today that he would not have let Sparta–Ajax go for anything.

'I know,' said De Goey, shrugging his shoulders shortly before the birth, when I asked him about it. 'If the match clashes with the birth then it's a shame for Feyenoord. I'll play other European matches in my life. I don't care what the coach, the players or the fans think of it. If I have to choose, I choose the birth. Actually, I wouldn't even call it a choice.'

In the end De Goey's son, Davey, was not born on the day of the match. Feyenoord, with Ed de Goey in goal, were knocked out.

When Ed de Goey still lived with his parents, he traditionally dusted the top of the cupboard for his mother. When I interviewed him at home in Gouda in 1995 he had just finished hoovering. Ed de Goey is one of the few emancipated footballers.

In his house in Gouda he not only hoovered, he fed the Persian cats JJ and Jason, gave his son a bath, went shopping (Ed turned out always to have a guilder on him for the supermarket trolley) and he filled and emptied the dishwasher.

Just before Chelsea won the Cup-Winners' Cup I read that the players don't think De Goey is a very sociable guy. Always first to disappear after practice, that kind of thing. I experienced a *déjà-vu* when I heard it. I thought: he has remained himself.

In 1995 I asked De Goey why he always left first after practice. The Feyenoord players didn't regard it as evidence of much team spirit.

'I just never eat at Feyenoord,' said De Goey casually. 'I eat my sandwich here at home. Here I am happy. I have a fantastic wife. With her I can get rid of my problems. She understands me. Also when it has to do with football, because she knows a lot about it. One thing is for sure: my family comes first, and only a long way after that comes football.'

He began to explain without caution that and why he doesn't fulfil the image of a professional footballer: that he's not a macho, that the football world does nothing for him, that he regarded keeping for the Feyenoord first team as work, that the glamour means nothing to him, that he is someone who likes to stay in the background, that he feels happiest there and that he goes home as soon as the match is over and that the people who don't like that don't interest him.

Gianluca Vialli and De Goey's colleagues may have found the keeper guilty of lack of involvement, may even have found him unsociable, but they mustn't forget that they have very different principles and place very different demands on life. For instance, have they considered that happiness can be minimal and one-dimensional: that you put the key in the lock, turn it, and know: here you will find your happiness. I think that lots of footballers can't imagine that you can be very happy with the woman you are married to. Ed de Goey desires no other women, doesn't care for a flamboyant life outside football, would rather walk around in a tracksuit than in a tailored Versace suit and brings peas back from Holland, because he doesn't like the ones in England much. What I want to say to everyone who will work with the touching Ed de Goey in future: for God's sake leave him alone.

I am tempted to write that the free-kick taken by the Brazilian Branco during the World Cup football in America of 1994 changed De Goey's life, but that is blatantly not true.

The quarter-final between Holland and Brazil was techni-cally and tactically of a rare standard. Holland was losing 2-0 and I remember that I wasn't sad about that because after four weeks of America I was being eaten up by homesickness. When Dennis Bergkamp and Aron Winter evened it up for Holland I was torn. Away from my wife and Holland for even longer, I don't think I'd have been able to stand it. Holland attacked.

Branco's free-kick.

Even today De Goey still insists that it wasn't a goalkeeper's error. The camera behind the goal shows how the ball passes between Valckx and Romario. De Goey anticipates a deflection. Only when he sees that there will be no *carambole* does he finally reach for the ball which has been kicked in the typically Brazilian way and is moving in from outside. Even if it is only by a fraction of a second, De Goey is too late. 3-2. Holland are knocked out.

Dick Advocaat, the coach, and Pim Doesburg, the goalkeeping coach, spoke straight after the game of a keeper's error. A top-class keeper can make as many mistakes as the keeper of a veterans' team, but the moment those mistakes are decisive the keeper has had it. Until then De Goey had never made keepers' errors that influenced the result.

I still think De Goey is a very good keeper, but he lost a lot on 9 July 1994. A lot: his status as one of the best keepers in the world, his place in the Dutch team, his magic. His magic: I remember saves and reflexes during Feyenoord matches that were so unreal that one suspected he was superhuman, or that God or Yashin was whispering in his ear at the moment a forward shot or headed.

And do you know what: I have never had the feeling that Ed de Goey feels burdened by that 9 July 1994. For a lot of keepers, life would have become unbearable. Not for Ed de Goey. That one free-kick from Branco didn't change his life, but just gave his career another twist. Not Pim Doesburg, the man who discovered and formed him, but Antoinette, his everything, helped him deal with the blow.

When I visited Ed de Goey at his home in Gouda in 1995 I was surprised. Incidentally, you have to imagine the interior of the house as follows: white tiles, white walls, white ceilings and white planks, and some cheap black reed chairs. Antoinette, who had borne him a son a couple of weeks before, was sitting on the sofa, with the Persian cats JJ and Jason beside her. In that ambience De Goey recovered from falling down and standing up. He was indescribably happy there. I saw it myself. I noticed it because I had never seen footballers do it before, but Ed de Goey kept shooting glances of love at his wife.

Oh yes, and now the story about my friend who is walking on the beach with his greedy, lazy, argumentative wife.

'You see that tall man over there?' he asks this annoying woman whom he keeps forgetting to dump.

That cow with the eternally wronged, irritable face walks barefoot through the cold, dirty water of the North Sea. A hundred metres in front of them a couple are walking hand in hand, a tall man and a short woman. 'Do you recognise him?'

She is silent, because of course she doesn't intend to make up, she is going to let him wait and suffer another couple of days, even though she had provoked the row like a pro.

By the sea you find, in winter or in summer, two kinds of married people. Those who have just had a fight and have to talk about it urgently, and those who are in love and still unaware of the fact that in future they will often row and have to talk about it. My friend and his annoying bitch belong to the first category, Ed and Antoinette to the second.

'That's De Goey,' he says.

Of course she doesn't look up.

At that moment he sees how Ed lets go of Antoinette's hand, throws his arm around her and presses her awkwardly to him.

His own wife was probably to blame for it, but that intimate scene filled him with an emotion that had always been foreign to him and which he had always despised, jealousy. At the same time he was moved. He could not believe that there are footballers who treat their wives with such tenderness, love and respect.

Sections of this article previously appeared in Hard Gras, *the Dutch literary football magazine.*

i don't fancy dennis bergkamp

HARRY RITCHIE

'*Jingle bells, jingle bells, jingle all the way. Oh what fun it is to fuck the Pars on New Year's Day.*'

It is 1 January 1982, or maybe 1983. Raith Rovers are beating Dunfermline Athletic (that contradiction in terms) 6-0 in the big Fife derby and I am a very happy young man. Not only are we Raith fans going mental because we're beating the Pars 6-0, I've managed to recover from my Hogmanay hangover with the help of some very stiff whiskies, I'm looking forward to the traditional New Year's Day meal after the match (potted heid, steak pie with mashed potatoes, black bun with cheese) and I'm watching this magnificent trouncing with Anne, whom I love and adore. What could be better?

Well, one thing which could certainly be better is Anne's attitude. Quite frankly, her initial enthusiasm for this match seems to have been gradually replaced by a desire to be not here. Indeed, I suspect that it is only the imminent threat of the traditional New Year's Day meal (potted heid is a stringy meat paste, black bun looks a bit like Christmas pudding but one modified to contain twice the calories and a thick pastry crust, and both dishes, even I have to concede, are acquired tastes) that is keeping her by my side.

'What's the time now?' Anne asks.

Three minutes after you last said that, is what I think to myself, but what I say is 'Four thirty-five. Five minutes left. FUCKSAKE REFEREE!'

Insert, if you will, a Pinteresque pause while, on the pitch, some numpty Dunfermline defender gets away with grievous bodily harm and lumps the orange ball upfield. Finally, she says it.

'Can we go now, please? I mean, they are winning five-nothing.'

'Six-nothing. GET INTO THIS SHITE, RAITH! The last few minutes, Annie.'

'Yes, but . . . it's snowing even harder. And I don't seem to have any feeling left in my feet.'

I am a man of tenderness and empathy. And this is a woman I really do love. 'Just a couple more minutes,' I tell her, and gallantly move a yard towards what might be, under the snow-drift, the edge of the terracing.

'He's blond. He's quick. His name's a porno flick. Emmanuel. Emmanuel.'

It is 3 May 1998 and I am in a pub in Highbury. It's one of those new-fangled pubs that are apparently modelled on the Central Perk coffee-shop in *Friends*. There's even an old leather chesterfield in the corner. Tonight, though, the usual studenty clientele have had to go elsewhere and nobody is ordering any of the excellent Thai food because tonight the pub is packed with Arsenal fans celebrating the 4-0 win over Everton which has clinched the championship.

Always one to avoid the stereotype of middle-class chaps who work in the media and live in north London, I have, over the past few seasons, become increasingly fond of Arsenal. I am not, and never will be, a fully fledged Gooner, and when the Arse play Raith in the European Superleague, I will feel not the slightest qualm about joining the Away supporters at the Clock End and bawling the Rovers to victory. So I am sympathetic to, rather than an integral part of, the pub's joyful pandemonium.

All season, and especially tonight, I've felt rather like a member of the Stasi who has been invited to sit in on a policy meeting of the KGB.

This could not be said of the dozen other people at my table – or, to be accurate, on and under the table. Gooners all of them to a man, and a woman. And that's the thing because included in this particular group of Gooners are two women – Mary, born and bred in Islington and a lifelong Arsenal devotee, and Amanda, a sporadic fan for a decade and season-ticket-holder for two seasons but someone who preaches the faith with the passion of the recently converted. Here they are, drunk, ecstatic and piping out, in ear-splitting soprano, the new songs about Arsenal's French midfielders – the porno-flick homage to Petit, and now the Gooners' cover version of 'Volare', complete with the rarely used third line: 'Veeyera, oh oh. Veeyera oh oh oh oh. He comes from Senegal. He plays for Arsenal. And Spurs will win fuck all. *Vee*-yera . . .'

One of the heartwarming sights in recent seasons at Highbury has been the increasing number of black faces in the crowd, and the increasing number of women kitted out in shirts carrying the JVC logo. Of course, Arsenal are unrepresentatively trendy, and I'm sure that non-white and non-male people feel as uncomfortable as ever at somewhere like the New Den. But it is an obvious truth that the nineties have witnessed an enormous growth in the number of women who are into football and go to games – a symptom and probably in turn a cause of the far more civilised atmosphere at grounds now compared to what daft nostalgics insist were the golden days of the seventies, when the football was far more naive, the pitches were mudflats, the stadiums hadn't been updated since the heyday of the industrial revolution, and there was the ever-present threat of some bullet-headed youth rearranging your groin with his knee-high Doc Martens.

Along with the increased availability of salmon and the triumph of social democracy, the growth of women's passion for football is one of the tremendous boons of the nineties. I find it a real joy to discuss our mutual hatred of Rangers with Mary, to listen to Amanda defend the slow-witted runs of Nicolas Anelka. Granted, celebrating Arsenal's championship would have been a far more amenable experience than vibrating with cold at Raith's 6-0 victory fifteen or sixteen years ago, even if Amanda and Mary weren't here, and it's not as if I had to explain to Anne why the outfield players weren't passing the ball by hand. Nonetheless, it's too tempting in this north London pub in 1998 not to think back to that time when watching a football match in the company of a woman was like bungee-jumping – a one-off event, filled with anxiety and fear.

I'll add one other point before rampant sexism rears its ugly head, which is to pay tribute to the certain amount of resolve women still need to attend a match. Even at (relatively) trendy, well-heeled Arsenal or 'family' clubs like Charlton and Norwich, women will be in a conspicuous minority and surrounded by all manner of un-gentle men prone to, for example, a possibly offensive overuse of the c-word. White British men aren't often given the opportunity to experience what it's like to be in this sort of conspicuous minority. I can think of only a few occasions when I have been given an inkling of what that feels like. There was one time when I was in Hong Kong and it dawned on me that in an otherwise packed tram I enjoyed a good space all to myself because, I was told later, to the local Cantonese I stank of rancid dairy produce. Then there was that night when a gay woman pal took me to a Soho bar whose customers consisted of two other men and perhaps three hundred lesbians. On both occasions I felt anything but at ease. Actually, on both occasions I had to remind myself that I was in no evident physical danger and that I ought to keep breathing.

'There's no point in going on.'

It's a day after Arsenal clinched the Premiership title and Richard Keys is having to wind up this Sky Sports broadcast early. This is because Richard Keys, Sky's usually unflappable answer to Des Lynam, has completely failed to cope with a fit of the giggles brought on while he attempted to provide commentary on the very brief highlights of the Women's FA Cup final between Arsenal and Croydon. I missed the particular incident which set Richard Keys down the path of uncontrollable laughter, but I'd already winced at enough embarrassingly inept play to infer that, whatever happened, it was undoubtedly a hoot.

To get this into proper perspective, the sight of, say, the Arsenal Ladies' goalie panicking at a high cross was a hoot only because Richard Keys and I are accustomed to watching games featuring incredibly skilful, full-time athletes. In the unlikely event that I ever play for Arsenal Ladies or Croydon, I'd last about two minutes before hobbling off the pitch to a chorus of my team-mates' jeers. And one of my cherished memories of last season was Andy Gray showing an action replay from some charity kickabout at Wembley, when Richard Keys discovered that, by some strange error, he had been put through one-on-one on the goalkeeper; first he dithered, then he panicked, then he accelerated to a slow walk and finally, having just avoided committing a professional foul on himself, he cunningly tapped the ball into the keeper's hands.

But having said all that, I should be candid and admit that, despite my better intentions and just like Richard Keys, I ended up ashamedly scoffing at the Women's FA Cup final – not just because of the bungles but because, deep down, in a recess of my mind that I usually try very hard to ignore, there's a little part of

me that refuses to accept that any woman's experience of football
– playing the game, supporting a team, watching a match on the
telly – will be as valid, as full and as genuine, as any man's.

Partly because Anne is a veteran not only of the Stark's Park
blizzard but of the radical feminism of the early eighties (an era
of Reclaim the Night marches and the invention of pronouns
such as s/he), I did have to steel myself to write the preceding
paragraph. And I'd like to add, straight away, that my confession
at least possesses the virtue of honesty, and, moreover, that I can
back it up with reference to the extensive research I have
conducted on this subject, research consisting of conversations
with male friends who both admitted that, deep down, they also
felt there was something not quite right about female football
fandom.

Awkward though it was to bring this sexism out into the
open during those two conversations, it was, as Ruud Gullit
would say, also funny also – having the same naughty, smirky
effect as the selective and knowing use in all-male chat of the
collective noun 'minge'. So far, so comforting, but it was only
when I started to ponder the reasons for this condescension that
I began to feel less comfortable – in fact, I began to suspect that,
as with any confrontation I've had with any woman ever, I was
going to end up losing an argument of my own making. Having
asked myself what exactly were the differences between my full
and rounded, masculine experience of football and that of many
women, most women, the vast majority of women, women, I
came up with answers that were either disconcerting or horribly
galling.

First of all, there is an undeniable discrepancy between my
passion for football and that of Mary and Amanda, in that I just
don't fancy Dennis Bergkamp. Or Ian Wright. Or Emmanuel
Petit. Even Nigel Winterburn fails to ring my bell. (Steve Bould,

though – now there's a saucy piece of work.) Acknowledging
that heterosexual women may feel a certain tingly frisson at a
football match that I have never felt, and am unlikely to feel until
Kylie Minogue signs for Raith, seems easy enough at first. What,
for goodness' sake, does sex really have to do with the far more
important business of football? But each time that Bergkamp
runs towards the touchline and that bit nearer to her as she sits
in the Lower East Stand, and Amanda's face is transformed into
a mask of lust, it serves to subvert a couple of delusions that I –
and many men, most men, the vast majority of men, men –
nurture and cherish.

You see, each time a female fan does something like comment on Dennis Bergkamp's legs, it's not so much a blow to the
male ego as a pinprick, but a pinprick that punctures a daftly
inflated self-image and sends it farting skywards. Women look in
the mirror and see a ghastly collection of imperfections; men
look in the mirror and see – quick, quick, suck in the stomach –
well, hello . . . a bit of all right. Okay, fair enough, maybe we
could lose a few pounds but if we went to the gym and drank a
bit less and got a decent haircut and tried some facial lipo-
suction, we'd make Dennis Bergkamp look like Tony Adams.
Easy. Well, that's how I normally think but it's only when
footballers become the object of well-informed female desire that
the truth dawns – even after an arduous and hyper-expensive
makeover, I would make Tony Adams look like Leonardo di
Caprio because Tony Adams is much fitter, healthier, younger,
richer and – heaven help us – better-looking, and infinitely more
famous, talented and charismatic, than me.

Call me an unusually dim klutz if you will, but I wouldn't
have written any of the above if I didn't know that my
preposterous vanity wasn't typical of my gender. To appreciate
just how stupidly deluded ordinary men can be about their
physical prowess, all that's needed is to spend a few minutes

eavesdropping on male fans' match commentaries. Which mainly consist of laments, complaints, sighs, groans and abuse – directed not only at the officials and the opposition but the players in their own team. Why? Because male fans believe, profoundly and unshakeably, that they could have done much better. Why didn't Lee Dixon continue his overlap? That's what we would have done. See how Keown just hoofed that clearance into the crowd? Why didn't he slip a pass through to Overmars, available and unmarked, a mere fifty yards away? Tcch.

Football is a deceptive and difficult game to play but it is also simple and natural and doesn't require its participants to be, for example, eight foot three or capable of punching another human being to a state of insensibility, although the latter quality might help if you want a trial with Airdrie. Conveniently mislaying all memory of the game's real difficulty, male fans react to each mistake, each fall from the grace of 100 per cent perfection, with the impatience and frustration of a highly strung Nobel prizewinner trying to teach superstring theory at a creche. Whereas someone like Mary, who has never really played football, is left to marvel and admire and gasp in awe as Keown averts danger by swinging a perfectly timed boot at the ball and sending it high, high into the top tier of the North Bank.

Moving swiftly on from matters physical to a higher, one might almost say spiritual, level, we arrive at the initially far more promising topic of what it is that women football fans lack – and what they lack is a definitely, defiantly masculine brand of knowledge and experience. Ask any woman fan to name Darlington's ground or the winner of the 1950 World Cup or the name of the gang of casuals that supported West Ham and you will get not the impatient, finger-on-the-buzzer response of any self-respecting bloke but a who-cares? shrug.

So there, I thought to myself, before the obvious fact occurred to me that this undoubtedly gender-specific ability to recall the nickname of Falkirk (bzzz – the Bairns) or Falkirk's highest home attendance (bzzz – 23,100, against Celtic, 1953) amounts to no more than nerdiness, and nerdiness is, I'm afraid, an exclusively masculine perversion. (Name me any sane girl who collects things, card-indexes them and arranges them in chronological or alphabetical order. How many women have you seen standing at the end of a railway platform, equipped with a notebook, camera and flask, and accompanied by an asylum orderly?) Football nerdiness, though, is of a peculiarly macho nature, since men who would scorn the knowledge that Paris is the capital of France as a self-evidently cissy accomplishment cannot afford to lose face among their mates by not knowing that Grimsby actually play in Cleethorpes. (I still shudder about once forgetting, for a moment, the names of Celtic's scorers against Inter Milan in the 1967 European Cup final, and I am truly abashed now at not being able to state, off the top of my head, which year in the early eighties began with Raith hammering Dunfermline 6-0.)

Which leaves only that vague mention of the masculine experience of football to support this rapidly crumbling argument, and what that vague mention really refers to is the primitive, adrenaline-fuelled tribalism which afflicts men far more than women at football matches. My apologies for citing another example from Arsenal's Premiership run-in, but I can't help recalling the two spectators picked out by the camera as the Gooners celebrated that crucial 1-0 win away at Man U – the first was a curly-headed bloke, the second a nice-looking girl. Both had adopted remarkably similar poses, performing imaginary pull-ups with clenched fists, but the TV director chose to concentrate on the nice-looking girl, not only because this was yet another instance of a capitalist patriarchy exploiting the image of a nice-looking girl but because she looked like she really was lost in bliss; she wore the expression of one who has just been told that, contrary to expert medical predictions, the operation was a success and, by the way, it'll be Mel Gibson who will hand over the outsize cheque for the Lottery jackpot. The curly-headed bloke was, by contrast, wide-eyed with the manic and scary frenzy of a man roaring defiance while sprinting into battle.

Hmm. Even under the duress of losing an argument, I don't want to end up boasting about the masculine capacity for aggression. I do sometimes feel resentful that women supporters tend not to have any direct experience of being chased by bullet-headed youths and tend not to be driven to extreme loathing of the opposition (I mean, Dunfermline Athletic and Rangers really are up there with Margaret Thatcher and Jeffrey Archer in my personal demonology), but I refuse to pursue this point because it's silly and I can see that it'll lead nowhere save to the admission that men are better than women at being violent and that men are better than women at getting their emotional priorities completely skew-whiff.

So female fans are less nasty than male ones, less paranoid and boring about football stats and trivia, less inclined to moan at imperfect play, because they are far less prone to the delusion that they themselves are pretty bloody tremendous, and many female fans can bring to the experience of watching football a carnal edge in their commitment that is noticeably absent in most male fans.

Having reluctantly acknowledged all these grim truths, wouldn't the logical conclusion state that football crowds would be much better if 90 per cent of the people in them had wombs?

Ah, you see. No. Absolutely not. No way. A nine-tenths female crowd would undoubtedly be more appreciative, emotionally mature and civilised, but think of the noise that crowd would make. Recall the shrill racket at a schoolboy international or, more shattering still, the constant, high-pitched screaming of

80,000 schoolgirls at women's hockey internationals at Wembley, and it's painfully obvious that an essential requirement for a raucous crowd which won't cause bleeding from the ears is that most of the people in the crowd should be tenors or basses. It might not be much, this marvellous ability of men to bellow, but it's the only source of masculine superiority I can think of and I reckon it's my duty as a man to make the most of it.

One other plus point: this is the only occasion I've taken part in an argument involving women without conceding defeat in a huff.

Aha! Not quite. There's still just enough time to stomp off in a sulk.

in broken french

SIMON KUPER

It was Sunday 4 October 1992, the day Lazio played Parma in the Stadio Olympico in Rome.

I had a peculiar job at the time, travelling around the world writing a book about football (*Football Against the Enemy*; 'now and then dips alarmingly into the bathetic' – *Sunday Times*). Sadly, my budget for the whole year was just £5,000. I had no money for match tickets, and so I had written to Lazio from Budapest to ask for a press pass.

That Sunday morning I turned up at the Stadio Olympico. I have learned one thing in life: when you turn up somewhere and say, 'My name is on the list', your name is not on the list.

'Your name is not on the list,' said the young Lazio official in charge of press tickets. I told him the address to which I had sent my letter. That had indeed been the Lazio headquarters, he said. But not since 1963.

I began to cry a little (after all, I was only twenty-two years old). The official's eyes filled with tears too, but he could not help me. I trudged the few hundred yards from the stadium back to my youth hostel. It looked like a Bulgarian beach hotel, there were too many guests, and few of them flushed the toilet after use. In the canteen I was served the worst meal in Italy.

I chose a table with a view of two French girls. We can swiftly pass over Virginie, a petite wavy-haired brunette in a white blouse. Next to her sat Isabelle: long, black curly hair, features from a Greek vase, and the posture of an Amazon queen. Somehow – and these things are always hard to explain – I felt attracted to her. Sitting with Isabelle and Virginie was an American moron. After a few minutes his chair fell over, and he came striding up to me.

'Hey,' he said.

'Hey,' I said.

We swapped names, autobiographies and route plans. Then the American moron, whose name I had already forgotten, said: 'I suggested to Virginie and Isabelle that we move to a place in town. They told me to find a buddy, so that we could get two double rooms. Will you be my buddy?'

'OK,' I said.

Then I returned to the Stadio Olympico, spent two days' food on a ticket, and saw Lazio beat Parma 5-2. Gazza played brilliantly.

That evening we found a small hotel in the centre of town. There were no double rooms left, so the four of us shared a small dormitory. I slept in the bed by the window, with the American moron next to me, Virginie next to him and Isabelle in the far corner by the door.

I had set off on my travels with the intention of working extremely hard every day. Until Rome, I had been tough on myself. In two months I had taken just three holidays: a week each in Berlin, St Petersburg, and Prague. In Rome I was going to work, because from Moscow to Barcelona I had lain awake at night in fear of bad reviews. That would mean I would never be able to go out in London again.

So the morning after Lazio–Parma I invested in the *Gazetta dello Sport* – '*E il morte di catenaccio*', it said about the Lazio match – and went for a quick breakfast with Isabelle, Virginie and the American moron. We found a table on a terrace in a sunny, fourteenth-century street. The American moron talked to Virginie, she read *Libération*, and Isabelle was left to me.

Isabelle was twenty years old, came from a Catholic village in the mountains near Grenoble, had a strict father, and was studying something in Lyon. She had met Virginie on holiday once, and they had clicked immediately. Isabelle spoke flawless English.

My task that day was to arrange my interviews. This was tricky in any country. You needed a telephone, coins to put in the phone, some unexpired phone numbers, and enough grasp of the local language to get past secretaries. The latter was particularly tough in Lithuanian and Estonian.

'Why don't you come to the Colosseum with us?' said Isabelle.

We wandered around for two hours, and when we finally found the Colosseum we discovered that tickets cost £7. The American moron and I had already hunched our shoulders and begun slouching away when Isabelle called us to attention. 'We'll just climb in over that fence there,' she said, pointing almost vertically upwards.

The American moron and I laughed foolishly. But seconds later Isabelle and Virginie were hanging ten yards high in the fence, and we had to follow. Isabelle and Virginie thought the Colosseum was fantastic.

That afternoon we hung around Rome and did lots of free things. In the evening we went to a bar. The American moron ordered a round of beers, and said he had some bad news. He had to leave for Greece immediately. He was supposed to meet a friend there on 9 October. It might have been 9 September – he was no longer sure – but in any case, he had to go.

Isabelle and Virginie were welcome to come along, he said. However, they declined.

The next day the American moron left the hotel well before noon. He had just a day and a half in which to buy his train ticket, a task for which backpackers usually reserve up to a week.

Isabelle, Virginie and I wandered through Rome. In a park, beneath a large tree that gave shade, we found a table. For hours we sat at the table and talked about life. Isabelle and Virginie laughed at my jokes. It turned out that we were all planning to go to Venice, and we decided to travel together.

The next day I had an interview with the sports editor of a Roman newspaper, who had Marcello Lippi-like grey hair, an Italian suit and dazzling brown shoes. I had last had a haircut in Kiev, and my sports jacket carried impressions from my backpack.

We talked about the culture of Italian football. He pointed out the flaws in all my theories, but he was very kind.

At the end he asked: 'So, how long have you been a journalist?'

I smiled mysteriously.

'One day?' he asked.

I had no other interviews in Rome. That evening Isabelle, Virginie and I strolled through the streets again, too poor for a bar. It began to rain, and we huddled together in a doorway. The sun was slowly setting, a ring of medieval churches rose around us, and Isabelle stood pressed lightly but noticeably against me. Back in the hotel, I sat in the kitchen and counted how many sides of notes I had made on my trip so far. If I kept going at this rate, I calculated, my book would be seventeen pages long. I decided to go and lie on my bed and fret.

As soon as I entered the bedroom I noticed that something had changed. But what? It took me only a minute to spot it. The bed next to mine, vacated that morning by the American moron, now contained Isabelle. She was engrossed in *Libération* and did not look up. Virginie looked straight at me, and raised an eyebrow in the manner of Connery's Bond.

Although I had been travelling around the world writing a book about football, I had yet to speak to a single footballer or football manager. They were legends and they scared me to death. But in Venice I was to interview Helenio Herrera.

The man had managed Spain, Italy and France (not at the same time), had won European Cups with Inter Milan in the 1960s, and claimed to have invented *catenaccio*. He once said that in an Italian popularity contest he would finish behind Sophia Loren, 'but only because she has a better figure'.

Normally I would never have dared speak to him. But luckily the Herreras knew my old university friend Kate. One summer in the 1970s, they had for some reason spent a holiday in the house of her neighbours in Leeds.

'Do you know how famous they are?' I had asked Kate.

'Of course,' she said. 'Mrs Herrera is a leading fashion designer.'

The Herreras had invited me to lunch in their Venetian palazzo. The interview was to be the highlight of my book, because Kate didn't know any other football legends.

There was only one problem. Herrera spoke Spanish, French, Italian and passable Arabic, but I had not paid attention at school. Perhaps his wife would translate for us. I could frame the questions in my miserable French. Isabelle and Virginie advised against that.

'People who speak French think that people who speak bad French are stupid,' explained Isabelle.

However, she and Virginie were willing to help me. And so, on the night train to Venice, I found myself telling two enchanting Frenchwomen the life story of Helenio Herrera.

I told them about the young player with a heart condition

who was forced by Herrera to train hard on a cold beach, and who died the next day; about Omar Sivori, the Inter player who once turned towards the bench during a game and fired the ball straight at Herrera's head; and about the referees bribed by Herrera's Inter. I told them about *catenaccio*.

'*Catenaccio*?' asked Isabelle.

'An iron chain of defence. You know, *no pasarán*.'

Isabelle and Virginie converted my questions into Stendhalian French.

Meanwhile we were starting to worry. The train was due to stop in Venice at 5 a.m. But it was our rigid, almost military, custom to rise each day at noon. Waking up at five was inconceivable.

In those days I spoke a little Italian, enough to have rudimentary rows with waiters. This had impressed Isabelle, who thought it almost made up for the fact that she was better looking, more charming, intelligent and mature than me. Isabelle told me to ask the conductor in Italian to wake us at five.

I argued that this was a bad idea. The man was bound to refuse, because Italian men were nasty to foreign men. It was often said that a foreign woman could not travel through Italy alone, but it was at least as hard for a foreign man, I argued. So I wrote on an envelope, in broken Italian: 'Please wake us at five.' Isabelle and Virginie took it to the conductor. And at five on the dot he burst into our compartment.

In Venice Isabelle, Virginie and I sat in a café on a canal and watched the sun rise. They refined my questions for Herrera. We found a hotel on a hidden *piazza*, and each took long, soothing showers.

The Herreras' *palazzo* was the most beautiful private home I had ever visited. Mrs Herrera had designed it, and it was sprinkled with caricatures of Mr Herrera.

In his office he talked my head off in French for two hours. His wife did not translate, but I caught the gist of it (I think). His parents were from Andalusia, he said, but poverty had forced them to Argentina. Yet the family stayed poor, and so they moved to Morocco, where he had grown up with Frenchmen, Arabs, Spaniards and Jews. From there he had moved to Paris, and later he had invented *catenaccio*.

He had also invented training camps, he told me. He would lock up his players and take them on long walks and ask them if they were happy. They had to tell him everything. *'Une équipe, une famille,'* he explained. 'We always had one long table for the whole team. I would sit at the head, and we would talk: "How are you? How is your wife?" '

Mrs Herrera served us a perfect lunch. Although shocked by my jacket, she and her daughter Luna were kind and beautiful. I was given wine. Helios, the Herreras' son, was away at university in Bologna, and after a couple of hours at table I realised that I had become a surrogate child.

Herrera kept thrusting plates of food at me. 'Stop that!' said his wife. 'He's not one of your players.' Herrera looked cowed. Mrs Herrera poured me some more vintage red. 'Why don't you come and stay with us here?' she asked.

I thought about it. A few days in the *palazzo* would be comfortable and nutritious. It would add pages to my book. By now I too regarded the Herreras as family.

'The only problem,' I said, 'is that I am travelling with two French girls.' Maybe Mrs Herrera would invite them too. Isabelle, Virginie and I could live in the *palazzo* for years. We could convert Mr Herrera's study into our bedroom. We would become Venetians.

'What a shame,' said Mrs Herrera.

After lunch Herrera took my arm and led me through the narrow streets to the dentist. He seemed to recognise something in the situation, and began asking me about myself, as if we were going to play Juventus the next day. He advised me to marry soon.

Soon the wine took hold and I no longer understood a word of what he was saying. At 5 p.m. we said an emotional goodbye, and I never saw him again.

I walked back to our hotel. This was to be my last evening with Isabelle. But how was I to express my feelings for her, with Virginie with us all the time? The situation appeared hopeless.

In our shared room Virginie was lying in bed dressed in white pyjamas. She was ill, she said. Isabelle and I would have to manage without her, she added. Isabelle and I hit the streets. It was a warm Friday early in October. Neither of us had slept for thirty-six hours. We decided to buy some food in a shop. Between us we had 4,000 lire.

Suddenly, a bottle of red wine loomed up before us. Isabelle inspected the label.

'3,990 lire,' she said.

We bought it. Sitting on the pavement on the Piazza San Marco, we watched the sun set. We watched the wealthy people at the café tables around us, and wondered what they had in their lives, except for food and that sort of thing. We kissed. Some of the time, this job was all right.

Isabelle stared into my eyes. 'You know what I don't understand?' she asked.

'Go on,' I said.

'You spent five years at school learning French, but all you can say is *oui* and *non*.'

We began speaking French.

I don't know how, but after a few minutes a French sentence came to me perfect and complete, as if it had dropped out of the sky.

'Isabelle,' I said, '*voulez-vous coucher avec moi?*'

'*Non*,' she said. I was welcome to address her in the *tu* form, she added.

The next morning, at Venice station, we parted. I was going to Barcelona, and Isabelle and Virginie to France. We all felt sad, and Isabelle was crying.

I tried to console her.

She explained, 'I'm crying because I'm sorry I ever kissed you.'

I said a long goodbye to Virginie. She wrote their addresses in my book.

Two weeks later I was back home in London.

'How was your trip?' my parents asked.

'Fine.'

'Did you meet any nice people?'

'Yeah.'

A week later I received a letter from Isabelle. I have since lost it, but it boiled down to this: Isabelle had discovered, to her astonishment, that she couldn't stop thinking about me.

Unfortunately, a day later I lost my address book in the Underground. Never would I be able to answer Isabelle's letter.

A week later I was in Yaounde, capital of Cameroon, writing my book again. It not as much fun as Venice. There was civil unrest, and for a white man to go out at night was regarded as an unsupportable risk, like jumping off a cliff or driving on the Yaounde–Douala highway. So I spent every evening in the *Mission Presbytérienne* where I was staying, listening to the radio on the veranda.

As each day passed I thought of Isabelle more. But I had lost her address, and so I would never see her again. Every day in Yaounde I hoped that I would run into her. After a while I began hoping that I would run into Virginie.

One morning I set off to hang around pointlessly in the Yaounde post office. As always, the market sellers on the square in front of *La Poste* were happy to see me.

'*Le petit français!*' the cry went up. I forced my way past countless handshakes, proposals of marriage and beggars with terrible diseases into the post office. And there, behind the counter, was a complete set of French telephone guides from 1983. I had a *eureka* moment: somewhere in there was Isabelle's address!

Instantly I had a second *eureka* moment: her surname was Grenier! And she had grown up in a village called St Genis-Laval! It turned out that there was indeed a village called St Genis-Laval. And a Grenier family lived there. In fact, four Grenier families lived there.

I had another *eureka* moment: Isabelle's father was called Jean! There were two J. Greniers. I wrote down both addresses, jumped into a yellow Toyota taxi, and returned – too excited to talk to the various other passengers – to the *Mission*. There, in broken French, I wrote Isabelle the most sensual letter in English literary history. I chose one of the two J. Grenier addresses and caught another Toyota back to the post office.

'I want to send this letter to France,' I told the man behind the counter.

'I would advise against that,' he said. 'People here open letters going abroad, hoping to find cheques.'

'This letter contains no cheque,' I said.

'Then, *monsieur*, they will throw it away in bitter disappointment.'

Back home in London I posted the letter. I did not write my name on the envelope: if the address was wrong, I didn't want some stranger to know it was from me.

My journey continued via Johannesburg, Rio de Janeiro and Dublin. Nowhere, however, did I run into Isabelle. And one afternoon back in London I was lying on the sofa watching TV when my mother came home from work.

'Hey,' I said. 'What's for dinner?'

After a while I noticed that my mother was waving a piece of paper in the air.

'This is yours,' she said.

I snatched it from her hand. It was my letter to Isabelle.

'Did you read it?' I asked.

'Yes, of course.'

She told me I must have sent the letter in one of her company's envelopes. Somebody in France had sent it back. At my mother's office, the letter had been opened and read by a large number of people. One had recognised my surname, and passed the letter on to my mother.

Nothing in this chain of events surprised my mother. She has no notion of what is probable and what is not.

Isabelle! Perhaps you are married by now. Perhaps you don't remember me. It could also be that you don't read *Perfect Pitch*.

However, if you do happen to read this story, then feel free to get in touch. Please write to me

c/o Perfect Pitch,
Headline,
338 Euston Road,
London NW1 3BH.

This story is dedicated to the memory of Helenio Herrera. Names have not been changed.

familiar anonymous ecstasy

JULIA NAPIER

'Sports,' intoned the furry fifth-grade teacher. 'Sports were invented as a substitute for war.' The boys brightened and jostled: a confederation of naked knees and awkward ears. The girls waited for more revelations about these hallowed masculine contests. Their teacher (known only as David to his students) began anew.

'Human beings are basically violent selfish animals – hunters and gatherers foraging for food and other humans. Many, many years ago, before the Industrial Revolution, tribal warfare kept men occupied so that they didn't kill people in their own villages. When we began to live in organised capitalist societies, someone invented sports to quell men's violent urges . . .'

'What's to quell?'

'Jake, it means to pacify . . . to lessen. To keep people from killing each other. Now, instead of killing the neighbouring chief, or running down a rabbit and eating it in the forest, people began to play football – or soccer – or whatever. Without sports, civilised society couldn't exist.'

The boys fidgeted, invigorated by this story: each one now a lunchtime warrior and the innocent game of capture the flag a timeless battle. The girls flattened: some incredulous, some alarmed, their already too large and hairy fathers suddenly hunters raging across the backyard on Sunday afternoon. David leaned back against his desk.

'Football plays are just simplified battle plans – if you look closely.'

That was the proof. He loved to dispense such facts and theories (the kids called them Davidfacts). Parents didn't enjoy it so much. Every week he produced highly entertaining proof that: the model for the Mona Lisa was a man, Napoleon had been slowly poisoned by Josephine and her lesbian lover, the true cause of the Spanish War was an international skirmish over saffron.

Tippania (Tip or Tippi to everyone – hounded as 'Tippi Longstockings' on the playground and for that reason never seen with hair past her ears) usually loved Davidfacts – especially since they infuriated her mother. This particular one, however, didn't make sense; it even bothered her. She hated watching the smirky nudging boys as David extolled his theory. Tip loved sports: kickball, baseball, touch football. But soccer was her game. Her parents had signed her up to play in the city's first girls' league when she turned five because it seemed like a good alternative to day-care. And Tip had loved it, loved it right away. She coveted her uniform: a maroon tee-shirt with a soccer-ball patch sewn on the sleeve and her number (28) ironed crookedly on the back, plastic Mitre cleats, and an elusive pair of shin-guards with plastic sticks you could take out (and lose, of course). Mostly, however, Tip loved to play – the race to chase the ball down when it was nearly impossible to keep in bounds, the smack it made on the inside of her foot when she actually managed to pass, and the rare suspended moment in front of the goal when she shot with all her childish muscles into the net – or the goalie or the bushes.

Every Saturday at 8.30 in the morning, weary parents assembled the girls (their team was called The Great Dames) for the chaotic games against the five or so other teams in their league. The Great Dames' home field was near an orphanage at the edge of the city called The Methodist Children's Home. Tip loved to play there. She yearned to catch a glimpse of a real orphan on the grounds, but they rarely appeared so early in the day. The Methodist Children's Home was the scene of Tip's first goal against the dreaded North Stars: a left-footed shot that bounced off the post and nicked in. Goal.

It was clear early on that Tip was good, good enough to play centre-midfield and almost never come out. She felt a vague pride in not hearing her name called as the whistle blew for subs, but mostly she just wanted to stay in, to run more, to fall and get up. It was always thrilling and terrifying and different. She could only describe soccer as a good feeling. It felt good the way mint-chocolate chip ice cream tasted good: simple bodily pleasure. Practice was just as fun as the games: drills, scrimmages in dirty pennies, crab-soccer, relay-races, and orange slices afterwards from the team mother.

As she sat looking at David, Tip didn't understand how soccer could be a substitute for anything. It was just what it was. It was what she did. It was how she felt most herself. Though she never quite grasped the significance of this conviction, it was her secret, the key to her brilliance, the grace that distinguished her forever. Her unmediated devotion to playing soccer, and not to some abstract notion of the game, drew people to her in ways neither they nor Tip understood. Her life emanated from this one perfect pleasure, and so she became perfect to others – if only in those flying green seconds of pass and trap and goal.

Tip continued to play soccer. She grew into an accomplished (if not brilliant) student, a pretty (though not beautiful) young woman, and an exquisite soccer player. This is not to say that she was the most skilled or the most successful player anyone had ever seen. She got cut from the state team after two weeks of practice because the coach couldn't watch her play. On most days, she merely distracted him; but, on others, when she was really on, he wept all down his clipboard – and he cut her from the team. She was good enough to school two thirds of the other girls' (or boys or whomever) on the field, but she lacked the silent, feral instinct of a true striker. She inevitably screwed up set plays because they bored her, and she had trouble staying in position. But no matter where Tip was, she was wonderful. On attack, she relaxed before the nervous full backs and slipped almost apologetically past them: slipped, swivelled, doubling all of her joints as her hips rolled in an improbable undulant loll. Coaches often reproached their defences for having turned to 'Swiss cheese' before her diaphanous fakes, but it was more as if they just melted as she dribbled through.

She wasn't the best. There was just nothing like her. People regularly commented on the sidelines that she looked as if she were 'playing under water' and moving through some gelatinous bubble alongside her team-mates. Her moves themselves weren't complex or amazing. It was how she wore them, paraded them, that mattered. No one could take their eyes off her, though the refs learned early on to ignore her altogether if they wanted to call the game remotely well. Even when she lost the ball to a lucky victim or passed lazily or shot wide, everyone watched. Scoring didn't interest her that much, but the defence usually lost its mark under her Bermuda Triangle charisma, and some-one was always there to receive her steady passes. She did enjoy, however, the occasional full volley or header on an open goal: the twin thunk and swish of body to ball to net.

Such was the stuff her greatest goal was made of, scored her senior year in high school. It was a high-skied September evening at the public park where her school team practised every afternoon. This particular day was a Friday, and, as schoolwork didn't beckon, a few of the girls decided to stick around for a game of seven-on-seven with the boys team in the wide late-summer light. While both varsity teams did well in their respective leagues, the girls were truly excellent and the boys solidly average. This inequality equalised the field of play between the sexes, and the games were usually close. The rules were always the same: no goalies, no throw-ins, no penalty shots: a clean happy scrimmage-plus lots of tight flirtatious marking.

After about twenty minutes, things were zigzagging along: skins 3, shirts 2. Everyone was breathing hard with sprints and giggles in-between goals and come-hither slide-tackles. Right after the skins scored for the third time, the shirts won a corner. Tip could feel the goal coming as Molly waited to take the kick. She hovered calmly at the back post and hopped a few languid steps forward as the ball lofted towards the edge of the six-yard box. Greg, her marker, was already so hypnotised by the supple swerve of her feet that he left her alone and, instead, marked the post she had abandoned. As the other girls jockeyed and pushed, she took one more step to the right and soundlessly left the ground. Just before the ball flew directly into her abdomen, she swung to the left in a gorgeous swoop and sent the black and white object of her affection directly into the lower right corner of the goal.

It slayed the entire skins team, and the game ended immediately: a 'next-goal-wins agreement' that had never been agreed upon. The boys just evaporated in embarrassed desire. The shirts, used to playing in a mixed crowd with Tip, rolled their eyes in the boys' direction and began to gather up their things. A little dizzy from her victory, Tip chose to spend the last gusts of daylight taking a few shots on goal. While her friends chirped off towards the parking lot, Greg fiddled with his Adidas bag, wanting very much to leave; but he couldn't help watching her: three even steps, the right foot curling, unfurling, smack, and a lazy jog to the open goal.

'I'll play goal – if you want?' Greg asked indifferently.
'Sure.'

Tip was not unpleased. She had had a crush on Greg for a year, but this term they hadn't had any classes together, and she thought she'd lost her chance. Greg was a few inches taller than she, wiry, with curlyish-thickish brown hair and soupy molasses eyes. He was one of the best players on the boys' team, but he had wooed her as Nario, head of the Sharks in the previous year's production of *West Side Story*. Greg had never noticed Tip off the field. She was pretty enough. But he didn't really like short hair on girls, and her thin toned body disappeared under her clothes. He rarely watched the girls' team play, but, when he did, it was to watch Tip. Her body, in easy conversation with the ball, enthralled him. He wanted to play with her, to play next to her, to be near the girl she became on the field.

Tip worked him out as best as possible, shooting high and hard into the corners. Entirely in her element, she teased him by turning conventional penalty shots into coy one-on-one contests. It drove him mad to see her dribbling that sibilant dance towards the goal, and, after about five minutes, he came straight off his line, didn't see her shoot past him, and kissed her at the edge of the penalty box. They tumbled downwards, rolling several times until they rested at the mouth of the goal. Dusk had, by now, tinged the sky to near darkness. Greg despaired at the fierce grip of her sports bra, but Tip pulled it off with one salty hand and then tugged at her shinguards, exposing the sweat-softened pink of her calves. Their discarded Copas lay in a mock embrace by the post as the night darkened and closed.

Though they broke up a few months later (at the end of the season), Tip didn't realise that all of her relationships with men would be forever entangled with her sport. Even when she met someone off the field, he soon became devoted to her on-field persona. It began to complicate things. What originated as genuine affection soon warped into a strange mixture of worship, jealousy, and disappointment.

College was a particularly difficult time. Tip got scouted by many of the top Division I schools, but all of the coaches left her games perturbed or in tears. She was too distracting for the big time and ended up starting at a lesser Ivy League power. Tip felt relief at this demotion; winning the national championship meant nothing to her and playing on TV even less. The game would be easier and more personal on a less conspicuous team.

She had always enjoyed the immediate friendships provided by her many teams, but her college team functioned (or didn't) like a sapphic soccer sorority. Everything was team-oriented: practice every day from 3.15 to 6.00 followed by a communal shower, and team dinner at 7.00 in their own special dining hall. On game days, the women were required to eat breakfast together and clandestinely to tack inspirational posters and candy onto the lockers of their 'secret psych-up soccer locker buddy'. Tip didn't mind it very much in her first year. The team partied together after games, and she enjoyed the instant network it brought her on the large, competitive campus.

Tip's relationships with her soccer sisters began to founder early in her second year. Since few men turned out to watch the women's games, they were slow to discover Tip. But discover her they did. Homecoming weekend of her sophomore year, an entire fraternity stopped at the field in the midst of a pub crawl. They were already drunk and tired by noon, and the women's game seemed like a good excuse to collapse in the grass. The second half had just begun, Tip's favourite moment in the game: finally really ready to play with forty-five minutes left to enjoy. She was already having a good game, but the alchemy that turned her limbs to lambent instruments of wonder had occurred. Hovering near the halfway line, she trapped a goal kick with her chest (her favourite trap) but managed to pop the ball up as she slowed its force, headed it twice over two defenders, brought it sweetly to the ground, passed it off, received it again, hung the stopper out to dry, and was about to score when the sweeper took her out with one loud swipe from behind. Penalty. Tip always took their penalties for an obvious reason. It was all in the set-up: a slow walk to set the ball down, swivel, jog back, one long look into the doomed goalie's eyes, and an instep pass into the corner. It never failed, and the whole fraternity went to pieces. One of them made it to his feet and cheered: 'Number 13 we love you!' Some rolled and sobbed in the grass, and others passed out from the double intoxication of beer and Tip.

Nothing was ever the same after that day. Men swarmed their games and serenaded Tip from the sidelines. She received hundreds of supplicating emails and soon stopped using her account altogether. Her pseudo-normal relationship with a poetic distance runner disintegrated instantly under the testosterone cloud that followed her everywhere. Of course, some of the attention was flattering, but Tip had never wanted to be an actress, and she felt now as if she were performing at every match: a captive performer to a coercive audience. The wild adulation distracted her terribly, and all of her super soccer sisters soon began to hate her.

It had been sort of funny at first, and the other women imagined that they, too, had inspired the increased attendance at their games. They soon lost their delusions and privately, in groups after practice, gossiped bitterly about Tip's 'egotistical exhibitionism'. Tip dreaded going to practice, and started to dress in her dorm room in order to avoid the middle-school cold shoulder of her team-mates. She asked her friends not to come to her games and began to fake injuries in order to stay on the bench as long as possible. The trainer, Bill, a deeply friendly guy with a prodigious belly (great for taping ankles against), had a talk one day with her about the whole rumpus while ultrasounding her (not) pulled quad.

Bill had always had a harmless fraternal crush on Tip – he never watched her play to avoid complicating their friendship – but spent long hours nursing her various wounded parts, and he had grown to adore her good-natured honesty. She never giggled or bragged loudly about her hangovers, and he relished her genuine friendliness. She was also a serious Cardinals fan, as was he. Bill began to worry when she started faking injury. He continued working the green ultrasound gel over her thigh as he spoke.

'So this whole thing has gotten a little out of control, don't ya think Tippo?'

'What thing?'

'Oh, nothing, just the fact that 300 guys came out to watch you play last Saturday and chanted your name all through the second half. You're you and everything, but I can't imagine it doesn't bother you.'

Tip had been trying to remove herself piecemeal from the team. She hated to sit on the bench watching, but she still felt the pleasure of participation from the sidelines. Her parents had noticed that she sounded depressed on the phone and sent her a care package, but she didn't want to tell anyone about anything that was happening; the entire situation filled her with a nauseating sense of shame. Never before in her whole life had anything separated her from the pure play of the game, the as-good-as-taste feeling of moving in diagonals down the field, anticipating goalkicks, tapping the ball, sending it long. More than anything, she felt lonely, lonely for the familiar and anonymous ecstasy of playing. Tip said nothing, but she cried quietly into the gunk on her leg as Bill kept talking.

'It's not your fault, and you know it's bullshit. Just try to enjoy yourself. And cut the crap with this quad and your Achilles'.'

She did. The following Saturday, in an aggressively close game against Amherst, with a record 600 spectators in attendance, Tip ended it. In the thirty-seventh minute of the first half, fans roaring 'Tippania! Tippania!' Tip stopped the ball cold at the halfway line, bent sharply down, picked it up in her hands and walked off the field through the silenced crowd. The ref didn't blow his whistle, the coaches didn't protest, and her team-mates did not call after her. Tippania had left the field.

Tip stopped playing that day, that minute. She didn't know what to do but disappear, to step off the balcony and leave her frenzied suitors empty-mouthed. The change in routine itself was devastating. She stayed late in the library or went for runs, trying to fill the hours in some productive way, but she still heard the gallop of cleats and the high calls of 'mark your girl!' Her friends called and invited and chatted, but Tip was amazed with loneliness. She slept too much, survived on Cheerios, and walked for hours listening to her Walkman. But, as Bill had said, she was herself, and she gradually resurrected her sense of purpose and of contentment. She took a painting class the following term, and, though she had no particular talent as an artist, the simple up and down of it, the attention to shape and colour filled her with something vaguely like her lost love of motion. She made new friends and started dating a guy from another school.

Tip graduated from college, moved to Brooklyn with some girls from school, and worked for a few years at an architectural firm. Living with friends in one of the greatest cities in the world suited her just fine. She liked being a draftsman, she liked Manhattan's four-star frenzy, and she liked Brooklyn's shabby tranquillity. It was entertaining and new and perpetually lack-ing. She always felt the same loneliness and the sense that her off-field body was a half-body, a bloodless double. When she ran, she was struck by how weak and hollow her legs looked as they pumped and slapped the ground in a pointless race against loss. In a desperate act of hope, she signed up to play in a women's league and managed to enjoy several low-key Sunday games before two of her team-mates (individually) confessed their love for her. One of them, happily married with a toddler, wept at the corner caff table where she had invited Tip for coffee. Tip felt horror and guilt over the whole incident.

Incapable of doing kick-boxing or funk aerobics in a thong like the rest of her friends, Tip ran several times a week in the park in Brooklyn. As soon as it got warm, small pick-up games would compete for space in the frayed fields where she ran in the evening. She always stopped to watch and rest a little. Each side a loose confederation of Latin Americans, Africans, Europeans, and the odd American, played spirited casual games with discarded shirts for goals and no official language. She would hesitate, jealous to the tips of her fingers, envying them their casual scrimmage. She envied them everything. They manoeuvred and shoved, each in his own among his familiars. Entirely unnoticed by the roller-blading jogging passers-by, the men shed the stilted posture of life beyond the pitch and eased into motion. They played.

Tip stood at the edge of the field, dying to join them. Unable to stop herself, she walked towards them.

'Excuse me, could I play with you all?'

'You play?'

'Yeah, I play a little.'

Laughter from the two teams.

'Sure, play over here.'

They noticed nothing at first because no one passed to her. But Tip had waited too long for this moment and, craving the light touch of the leather against her skin, won the ball and scored.

Wonder, lips parting, imagine that, God – she's beautiful.

The guys began passing to her, making space for her arching runs from the outside, marking her close, risking real tackles.

For five or ten minutes, they played together. Her feet thrilled at the tap of the ball, her legs made quick and useful again. The guys played their own game, inviting her slight swift body into the fast-passing dance. And then, it slowly fell apart. They began to follow her, Tip's own play dictating the game itself. Horribly, they became hers, forgetting to make runs, leaving her unmarked, losing the game. All they wanted was to watch her play.

Tip felt the change on the field. It was like the transition from being drunk and happy to being drunk and sick. She was sick and frustrated and furious. She didn't want to be them, to inherit their knotty quads and wide flat chests; she wanted their random invisibility, their just-another-guy disguise.

The game slowed pathetically, both teams circling her like a childish game of keep-away, an almost aggressive longing fixed in the eyes of her betrayers. For the second time in her life, Tip stepped abruptly off the field. She walked quickly to the key chain she had dropped at the edge of the pitch, strode straight to the ball, opened the pocket knife and punched the blade into the cheap leather.

homage to eamon dunphy

SIMON HUGHES

Pop into your local high street bookshop ten years ago, and you'd have found 'Sport' downstairs hidden away in the basement, nestling between 'Religion' and 'Military History'. But now sport sells, and sports books have come out of the closet. Unfortunately, their celebrity 'authors' usually haven't. In an era when washing-your-dirty-linen-in-public programmes like *Vanessa*, *Kilroy* and *Esther* are booming, it is extraordinary that football stars can make so much money out of books that reveal so little. Employing ghost writers seems, in many cases, to guarantee that the book itself is a phantom.

Insomnia cures like *Ruud Gullit – My Autobiography* or *Alan Shearer: My Story So Far* shortchange the public with their 'I was fortunate to grab the equaliser' or 'we knew training would be tough' platitudes, and another unread Christmas present gathers dust on the shelves. 'Most football books should never be published,' declared Eamon Dunphy, author of the gem of the genre, *Only a Game*.

It is twenty-five years since Dunphy first began writing his spiky, engaging account of the 1973 season with Millwall. He begins: 'On the first day, you have the photo call, and everyone compares sun tans, and tells lies about the girls they've had' – a comment which has a resonance with the beginning of the cricket season, or any renewed venture for that matter. Later he analyses what makes the great Leeds side of the 1970s tick:

Every time you get the ball there is this pest pestering you. Driving you mad . . . It is like some fellow running up to your desk or work bench all day and sticking a pin in you then running away. The cumulative effect is drastic. By the second half you have had it with Jackie Charlton. You don't want to ever see him again . . . Leeds, when they have got the ball, can play. Brilliantly. But they felt that was how they destroyed teams. Not by football. But by that. They played football once they had destroyed them.

The prose has urgency, observation, information. It reveals things, provokes discussion. Instead of lazily recording events in the cut-and-paste style of most modern autobiographies. Dunphy analyses feelings, gets under the skin of the players, chips at the cement holding the team together:

When you share a job with someone in football, a relationship develops between you, an understanding that you do not have with players doing a totally differ-ent job. It's a form of expression – you are communicat-ing as much as if you are making love to somebody. If you take two players who work together in midfield, say, they will know each other through football as intimately as any two lovers.

Back to Leeds again: 'That would apply to Giles and Bremner, for example. It's a very close relationship you build up when you are resolving problems, trying to create situations together. It's an unspoken relationship, but your movement speaks, your game speaks.' Just as well. No one could understand the wee man, once described as five foot four inches of barbed wire.

Much of a pro's life is spent on the training ground, and

most, blindfolded by routine, have little to say about it. Dunphy is eye-openingly candid.

> We had a practice match today, with an awful lot of bickering. Mainly because we were playing the reserves whose prime object in life is to mess us up. And they do that by not sticking to orthodox positions – you get centre halves tearing down the wing, that sort of thing. They will sacrifice their own chances of victory to destroy our chances of getting a coherent strategy together. One or two will mutter 'I'm going to kick that bastard' out of sheer frustration.

Dunphy went on to become an enigmatic journalist and broadcaster, but, with rare exceptions, the art of football book-writing has lodged in a vacuum, particularly those toe-curlingly awful dressing-room diaries in which few have understood the detail the masses crave. A rare exception is Garry Nelson's *Left Foot Forward*, a mellow portrayal of life in the League's lower echelons, dwelling on the pain of rejection and the bane of Christmas Day training: 'The biggest effort put in today was the sprint to the showers.'

Left Foot Forward was a bestseller, and *Only a Game* (which sold a relatively meagre 30,000) is still in demand and is being re-issued by Penguin this year. Anyone who buys it will be suddenly aware of how grindingly tedious the modern big-name autobiographies are.

It doesn't help that most are written in pre-O-level English and that the really big stars of the game see their footballing life in mere black and white rather than glorious technicolour. Men like Shearer don't tell us why they're where they are because they don't know and have never bothered to fathom it out. They're just *there*, that's all. Shearer on his debut in the (old) first division: 'The moments building up to the kick-off were a bit of a blur and I remember shaking like a leaf when I ran out onto the pitch.' Shearer on being dropped by England: 'I was delighted with my entrance on to the full international stage so you can imagine how disappointed I was when I was not chosen for the next friendly against Czechoslovakia.' Shearer on success for Newcastle over Man United: 'Everything went right for us that day in a 5-0 victory and the Geordie fans roared their approval.' If Shearer played like he 'wrote', those same fans would be clamouring to be let out at the interval. To think that whole rafts of forest have been razed to print guff like this. I'd rather stare at a dead tree to be honest.

Star sportsmen have two common denominators. They are hopeless self-analysts, and they are generally intolerant of the less well-endowed. Few, therefore, make good managers. Chris Waddle's Burnley lurched from crisis to crisis last season, finally avoiding relegation by their toenails. Asked after the final face-saving match why Burnley had been far more effective in the latter half of the season, Waddle replied, 'Bloody hell, I don't know.' Not surprisingly, he was soon looking for a job.

You can't imagine Ruud Gullit queuing up at the job centre after his Chelsea demise, especially as he has two fast-selling books on the market. The latest, *My Autobiography* (actually written by the *Daily Mirror*'s Harry Harris) is bannered with 'The True Story Behind the Headlines' but it is nothing of the sort. Instead it is an opaque account of a voluptuous career, his years at Stamford Bridge shallowly regaled. The intricacies of the biggest story of all, his excessive wage demands and subsequent sacking, are glossed over – 'I mentioned a high figure' – even though the amount (£2 million net) is no state secret. 'Now I have left Chelsea,' he goes on, 'my affection for the club has not dimmed, even though certain individuals have been very unfair, if not cruel, to me.'

Who these people were, or what they did we are not told. Now that would have been genuinely interesting, but Gullit cares not to identify them in case of a possible backlash. Sport reveals character, the behind-the-scenes behaviour of the participants at times of stress saying more about the personalities than who they marry or what their sitting room looks like. From my experience, you have to risk upsetting a few people, to sail close to the no-go zone, to tell the real story.

I suppose the next turgid blockbuster will be *Gazza – Tears of a Clown*. I've got a better idea. Create an Oprah-style sports programme, where the stars come clean about their relationships, and kick off with Paul and Sheryl fighting it out in public. Now that would be worth £16.99 . . .

the first game

ROGER HUTCHINSON

On the last day but one of December, 1889, a twenty-one-year-old schoolteacher from Birmingham disembarked after a violent sea passage at the remote Hebridean port of Lochboisdale and looked hesitantly about him at a rocky landscape swathed in mist and bathed with mild winter rain. Frederick Rea had arrived on the island of South Uist to take up a position as headmaster of the school at Garrynamonie.

The local political circumstances surrounding his appointment need not concern us much, although they were significant at the time. Frederick Rea was the first Englishman to be offered such a position in South Uist, and the first teacher there who did not speak Scottish Gaelic. He was also, however, the first Roman Catholic since the Reformation to be given a headmastership in this intensely Catholic island, and as such his commission was widely applauded in the neighbourhood.

Rea arrived in a district which, although part of the United Kingdom, was more alien to most of the people of England and lowland Scotland than many parts of Asia, Africa, Australia and America. Far more British civil servants spoke Urdu than the language of the Hebrides. Few, other than the occasional bagger of deer and gaffer of salmon, were acquainted with the customs – or even the whereabouts – of this lonely place. Rea himself, when the South Uist School Board wrote to ask for his references, had no idea where Lochboisdale was, although he vaguely remembered applying and supposed it to be somewhere in

Scotland. When he was offered and accepted the job his friends and relatives laughed at him.

'It is not easy to realise in these days of the aeroplane, motoring, and of the many facilities for comfortable travel,' he would write in 1927, 'how people of forty years back looked upon such a venture as I contemplated – less surprise would be created nowadays if a person proposed to take a school post in Spain or Greece.'

And less surprise, he might have added, would have been created back in 1889 if Frederick Rea had taken a post in Delhi, Melbourne, Nairobi or Newfoundland. By any useful measure Rea was transporting himself to one of the remoter unassimilated colonies. In the census of 1891 – which was taken in 1890, the first full year of Frederick Rea's residency there – the School Board district of South Uist contained 5821 persons. Of those, no fewer than 3430 spoke only Scottish Gaelic. A further 2102 claimed themselves to be bilingual in Gaelic and English, which broadly meant that they had been taught some English at school, and just 289 were, like Rea, monoglot in English. The island's only link with the rest of Britain was a small steamer which wound weekly towards it from the port of Oban in Argyllshire. There was no mains electricity or water supply, no telegraph cable, and the postal system was dependent on the ferry. There were no manufactories of any kind. The people survived from fishing and from the subsistence agriculture of their crofts.

Frederick Rea was met off the boat by the local priest and chairman of the School Board, Father Allan McDonald. They walked three miles from the pier to Father McDonald's dwelling, and Rea, searching for cottages, peered through the dusk past large, isolated heaps of turf and stones and earth, at an apparently uninhabited landscape. At last he burst out: 'But where are the houses?'

McDonald pointed at the blackened heaps. 'Those are the houses,' he said.

It was an alien land, an incomprehensible place, a district almost unrecognisable as part of Britain. Just as younger men were best suited to the administration of the more intractable dominions, so only a young Englishman could have adapted to the position of headmaster at Garrynamonie School in 1890. And because Frederick Rea was a young man and had a young man's interests, he would change for ever at least one large part of South Uist's venerable and tenacious insular culture.

At the end of the nineteenth century South Uist shared with the remainder of the Hebrides and the mainland Scottish Gaid-healtachd an antique repertoire of sports and recreations. The island's children and adults played a form of rounders which they knew as 'Cluich an Tighe' ('the House Game'). They competed at a sport named 'Speilean'. Variants of this distant ancestor of baseball were known elsewhere in Britain and in North America as Bat and Trap, or Cat and Bat, or One Old Cat, or Two Old Cat, and most particularly in Lancashire and Yorkshire as Trap and Ball or Knur and Spell (with which last word the Gaelic 'Speilean' shared a common root).

The islanders played a form of pitch and toss which they knew as 'Spidean', and a type of quoits called 'Propataireachd'. Their version of skittles had been christened 'Leagail Sheagh-dair' ('felling the soldier'). The game which children in the south of Britain enjoyed as 'King' was called in the Hebrides 'Dhean-adair' ('Achiever', or 'Trier'), and took a pattern of one elected tyrant whose function was to 'crown' new allies by laying his hand on their heads as they dashed past him towards the line which marked the safety zone.

They swung poles from the rafters or barns and tried to shake each other off the wooden horse onto the ground, and called it 'An Lar Mhaide', or 'the floor-stick'. The boys wrestled ('carachd') and rode ponies on the ribbon of white strand which runs for twenty miles and more down the Atlantic coast of South Uist; and they tested their strength at 'Ciopan Dochart' by sitting opposite each other with the soles of their feet braced flat against their rival's, holding with alternate hands a stout stick, with which one attempted to pull the other to his feet. The small girls played hunt-the-paper, and created intricate rhymes to accompany the many steps of 'Iomart Fhaochag', the whelk game, and led their smaller siblings through the rituals of 'MacCruslaig s'na mucan' – MacCruslaig and the pigs.

And for as long as the spoken and written records of their history could recall, back through all the busy centuries to the time just 500 years after Christ when the first few Gaelic-speaking Scots had tentatively set foot in these Pictish lands from Eire, they had played the team stick-and-ball game of shinty. They did not call it that: 'shinty' was a mainland anglification. They knew it by its ancient Irish name of 'Camanachd', the bent-stick game, or more usually and colloquially as 'Iomain', the driving game.

Two days after Frederick Rea stepped gingerly onto Lochboisdale pier for the first time, shinty was being played up and down the turf swards of South Uist, as it had been on every New Year's Day within and beyond memory. Large stones marked out goals on the broad and grassy machair lands of the west coast. A ball was made of wood, or of worsted yarn wound stiffly together, or of horsehair, or even of peat. Trees were at a premium in South Uist, and so the shinty sticks ('camans') were often carved from tangles of dried seaweed, or crafted by folding tightly a strip of sail canvas. And then the game progressed, from dawn to winter dusk, with fifty or more on each side whooping and skirling up and down the unlegislated pitch, competing at a sport whose only rules were those established by tradition, whose only constitution was the goodwill of the participants, and whose only referee was the reluctant arbitration of men too old to play.

Within two decades of Frederick Rea's arrival in South Uist, shinty was no longer played there. One thousand four hundred years of deeply ingrained sporting tradition was wiped like chalk from the face of the island. It was not destroyed maliciously, nor even deliberately. Shinty was simply supplanted, like a thousand of its distant relatives from Buenos Aires to Smolensk, by a game which was almost as young and innocent as Frederick Rea himself; a game which was travelling like some benevolent virus across the shrinking world in the kit-bags and carpet-bags and Gladstone bags of British soldiers, merchants, labourers, ministers of religion, and schoolmasters.

Frederick Rea was a keen sportsman. His personal predilection was for angling, a passion which was comfortably accommodated in the hundred fertile lochs of the southern Outer Hebrides. But he introduced his young charges at Garrynamonie School to many of the games of southern Britain.

He showed them cricket. One of his pupils, a woman named Kate MacPhee, remembered in later years how she and the other girls had watched jealously as the Uist boys were taught this fascinating sport, and then had practised on their own to the amusement of Mr Rea, who promptly arranged a match between the boys and girls – which the girls won, 'much to the chagrin and discomfiture of the boys . . . they drove us off the field in a shower of "pluic" [clods of earth] accompanied by shouts of "clann an diabholl" ["children of the devil"]. However, they were severely reprimanded by Mr Rea and were taught that such behaviour was "not cricket".'

Cricket did not catch on in South Uist. He introduced kite-flying, which delighted the children but alarmed an old woman who imagined that Rea was somehow hauling a large bird from the sky. He had a local joiner build parallel bars, which were installed on Wednesday evenings in the middle of the schoolroom floor, and he instructed the young men of the district, with a minimum of accidents, in a number of the new athletic disciplines.

Rea imported single-sticks and wickerwork head-guards for fencing exercises, with dreadful consequences. He first demonstrated cuts and guards, and then asked two pairs to engage each other . . . 'after fencing quite skilfully in a seemingly friendly manner, each pair began to slash at each other in great fury: the guards they had been taught were ignored and they dealt each other tremendous blows indiscriminately on body, limbs and head and such was the force of their blows that, in a few moments, the tough wood sticks were reduced to splinters with little remaining in their hands but the hilts.'

After that the headmaster was reluctant to produce the boxing gloves which had arrived by the same post. He finally found a use for them when two of the bigger boys were discovered beating each other senseless with bare fists in a corner of the playground. Frederick Rea strapped the gloves on them and told them to set to once more. 'Little damage was done', and they retired exhausted, shaking hands and grinning, while their peers laughed aloud at the wonder of it all.

And then one day – we do not know exactly when, but it was a Christmas holiday between 1891 and 1893 – two of Rea's brothers appeared in South Uist. They were both sergeants in a line regiment stationed in the Tower of London, and they were both keen soccer players. The Midlands home of the Rea family was a crucible of association football. Three of their local clubs – Aston Villa, West Bromwich Albion and Wolverhampton Wanderers – had been formed back in the 1870s, and had been among the twelve founding members of the Football League when it was launched in 1888 by a Scottish official at Aston Villa named William MacGregor. All three of these clubs were dominant forces in England when the Rea brothers arrived in South Uist to visit their teacher brother Frederick. West Brom and Wolves won the FA Cup in 1892 and 1893 before 25,000 and 45,000 fans respectively, and Villa were beaten finalists in 1892 and League champions in 1893-94. The fourth member of the Midlands quadripartite, Small Heath Football Club, was winning promotion as inaugural champions of the league's Division Two at the end of 1892-93. Small Heath would become Birmingham FC in 1905, and Birmingham City in 1945.

It is not surprising, then, that Rea's two soldier brothers took a football with them to Garrynamonie. They had not brought a pump, and so on the first fine day the three men sat in the schoolhouse sitting-room and took turns to apply their lips to the rubber valve and blow, until their lungs were aching and the leather panels were as tight as the skin on a timpano.

They then took the thing outside and introduced the game of soccer to South Uist. The three brothers booted the ball about for a while, smashing, to the schoolmaster's chagrin, a school-house window; and then a neighbour appeared, and the most classically colonial sporting cameo of them all was played out before the amused eyes of Frederick Rea.

'We invited him,' Rea would record three decades later, 'to join us; but he had never seen a football before and was nervous. I kicked the ball towards him and told him to kick it back; he walked to it, looked at it, and stood and grinned again – I don't know if he thought it would hurt him if he kicked it, but he stood there looking most embarrassed while we stood laughing at him.

'I went to him and gently kicked the ball two or three times with my toe; then I put it by his feet and told him to do the same. Very gingerly he touched it with the toe of his heavy boot. "Good," said I, retreating a few steps. "Send it to me"; which he did but very gently. After he had watched us three giving the ball some hefty kicks he gained courage and joined us, we played

a two-a-side game, with Sandy most enthusiastic but observant
of the rules about handling the ball.'

Two more Uistmen joined in, and it was agreed that on the
following day, a Saturday, they would all meet on the machair:
those level turflands which were the traditional home of winter
shinty matches. The three Reas made goalposts and carried them
down on the appointed hour, to find their friends waiting. The
posts were erected, the pitch was paced out, the three-a-side
teams were picked, and the game kicked off.

And then the occasion becomes, in the telling, suddenly
reminiscent of the appearance before Lord Chelmsford's be-
leaguered troops of Cetewayo's overwhelming Zulu impis at
Isandhlwana and Rorke's Drift. The six men had been playing
for about five minutes when a number of figures loomed into
view, black silhouettes against the winter light, marching
towards them . . . 'more and more appeared on the skyline
coming from various directions, scores of them. Sandy had given
the ball a mighty kick towards the opposite goal and dashed
after the ball, when the foremost of the newcomers rushed
forward and reached it first. He picked up the ball, ran with it,
then kicked it in the air.

'My younger brother trapped it as it fell, and we hastily
chose and arranged our two elevens from those of the newcomers. They seemed to understand Sandy's explanation of the
game, and that no one was to handle the ball but the one in
charge of the goal. The game restarted and all went well for a
few minutes until the newcomer players became excited – then
they would rush at the man who had the ball, catch hold of his
coat and hold him, while another player of his side got the ball:
the opposing men then rushed at this player and rolled him over
while he lay clutching at the ball.

'By this time more men had arrived on the scene, and
seething with excitement they joined in the game. My brothers

and I stood aside shaking with laughter, for there were now fifty-a-side at least; some were tearing about the field looking for the ball or rushing at each other, while in another part of the field a mass of men were rolling over each other, one of them wildly clutching the ball; if the ball came into sight again the excitement waxed furious, and the whole hundred or so men would dash after it, throwing each other down, tearing at each other, all in a mad effort to get the ball.

'Fortunately,' concluded Frederick Rea with the satisfaction of a District Commissioner, 'the ball came towards me, and I put my foot on it, held up my hand, and called out: "A mach!" ("Go!"). Perhaps hearing me pronouncing Gaelic sobered them, for they all stopped and I told them quietly that the game was over. Several helped with the goalposts, and we reached home thankful that no casualties had occurred.'

News travelled fast on South Uist, Frederick Rea would have cause to reflect. The next Sabbath day the queues before St Peter's Church in nearby Daliburgh were resonant with the single word: 'fooot-baal'. The young priest there, Father George Rigg, called the brothers into his house, told them of his own fondness of soccer in his college years, and suggested a properly organised match – on New Year's Day.

Only one man seems properly to have identified the thoughtless impertinence of this usurpation by the professional classes of the island's traditional shinty fixture. Frederick Rea bumped into the retired Daliburgh schoolmaster George MacKay shortly before the Big Match, 'and he sniffed as much as to say "What new-fangled idea is this?" '

Rea picked his side, putting the Eriskay priest and chairman of his governing school board, Father Allan McDonald in goals, he and his brothers in the forward line, and seven quickly coached local boys in the other positions. Father Rigg's side more perfectly represented the administrative bourgeoisie, including as it did two other priests, a college student on vacation, two clerks from the estate factor's office and an accountant from the bank. Father George – aware of what had happened on Garrynamonie machair that previous Saturday when the Rea brothers appeared with their ball, and determined that the game of soccer should not again be played like shinty in South Uist – also obtained as referee a captain of the Cameron Highlanders who happened to be staying at the Lochboisdale Hotel.

There was a big crowd for the first proper game of competitive football in South Uist, and they 'remained outside the playing pitch'. Frederick Rea's side played to the whistle – 'which was a lesson in restraint to the many young fellows who had followed us from our end of the island' – and wound up winning 3-1. The Rea brothers from Birmingham knew about the science of this game of soccer in the early 1890s, you see . . . 'if my brother on the left wing were tackled by several opponents, he swung the ball to me in the centre where I made ahead for goal, and, if pressed, I tapped the ball to my other brother on the right wing, thus combining our play; whereas the opposing side were individualists who, though good players and full of energy, wasted much effort.'

Only the old schoolmaster, George MacKay, was unenchanted. After the match 'he sighed as he wagged his sage head and said: "Ach, aye! But you and your brothers understand the game," and off he went without a further word.'

George MacKay may not have lived to witness the complete replacement by football of shinty and speilean and cluiche an tighe in the southern Outer Hebrides, but he certainly saw the beginning of their end. They lasted not much longer. And the scenes portrayed above could have happened anywhere, and did happen almost everywhere.

They were imperial scenes. Not the most harmful or distressing of imperial scenes, perhaps. The implantation of organised sports may indeed be the only commonplace deed of Empire which was not only willingly embraced at the time by the indigenes of the dominions, but which is still welcomed today.

But they were imperial scenes nonetheless, repeated on a hundred Indian maidans and all across the high veldts of Victoria's possessions: from the local interpreter explaining the rules to his neighbours, to Frederick Rea's tickled frustration with the 'excitable' natives, to the fact that one of those football-ing brother's bones would be left a few years later rotting in the sand at Omdurman; they were imperial scenes.

Soldiers and schoolteachers were the John the Baptists of the faith of association football and the hundred other recreational devices of the Victorian British; soldiers and schoolteachers and priests, and railway workers and miners and factory managers took them across the world in a few short decades, and when they had finished their work the world would never be the same again. By the time that they had collected their company pensions and retired back to Hertfordshire, Rutland and Loch Lomond-side, around the earth men and women played and watched and understood identical games, and so a huge international network of sport became suddenly possible: a network which would quickly evolve into an entertainment industry so massive and so important that it created untold millionaires and broke as many hearts; bred corruption, riots, manslaughter, murder and even wars; felled governments, dominated lives, and enriched the existences of countless ordinary people. Faced so surprisingly with the ground-trembling roar of this irresistible juggernaut, the idiosyncratic, sweet old traditional games of the village sward mostly took heart attacks in its headlights and died an unremem-bered death.

Empires require discipline and impose standards. Frederick Rea would reflect of his introduction of soccer to the schoolchil-dren of South Uist that 'the fairness of its rules seemed to appeal to the boys who played both with zest and enjoyment but with due observance of a penalty for unfair play'.

Five years before Frederick Rea was born, soccer had become a disciplined, codified, responsible game: a game which Victorian schoolmasters could not only enjoy, but could also introduce to their flocks with a clear conscience, happy in the knowledge that by playing football the boys were learning teamwork, restraint, fairness and the meaning of the rules.

A hundred years after those seminal soccer matches on the South Uist machair in the early 1890s, the visitor to that island who travelled with an eye open for sport would have seen effectively no facilities other than soccer pitches. Had that modern visitor stopped on the machair to watch a game, he or she would have been entertained by association football of a very high standard indeed, considering the small population of the place. The young men in the region of Garrynamonie School formed decades ago a football club called South End, which played in the Uist & Barra League. This league, which covered the sparsely inhabited islands of Berneray, North Uist, Benbecula, South Uist, Eriskay, Barra and Vatersay had between nine and ten football teams. The combined population of these islands was, in the census of 1991, just over 7,000. The population of South Uist and neighbouring Eriskay, which had been almost 6,000 in Frederick Rea's time, was reduced to just 2,285. South Uist and Eriskay nonetheless fielded in the early 1990s no fewer than four senior football teams. The game which conquered the world had also conquered the southern isles of the Outer Hebrides.

In 1993, in unwitting celebration of what was possibly their centenary, the footballers of South End FC – men with the surnames of Frederick Rea's pupils and neighbours, MacPhees, MacIsaacs and MacDonalds; men who still spoke Gaelic, knew Gaelic songs and stories and traditions; but men whose fathers had long forgotten the games of the past – enjoyed their finest hour. As champions of their local league they entered in a trans-Highland soccer cup competition whose first round draw included the names of more than 100 clubs from across the north of Scotland. After a number of trips over hundreds of miles of land and sea, and a series of scintillating performances, South End reached the final, where they were beaten in a blaze of goals and glory. Frederick Rea and his brothers would have been astonished.

'The Uist boys used to be,' wrote their compatriot Alexander Morrison in 1908, 'and in some places still are, very proficient at the game, the main qualities . . . being speed and dexterity.' The game that, in the 1900s, Morrison was already talking of in the past tense, was of course the game of "iomain", or shinty. Today, despite a small revival at junior level, hardly a single shinty stick had been used in competition in South Uist for the best part of a century. Sporting skills are easily transferable. As transferable as a young man's affections on New Year's Day.

disappeared

GRACIELA DALEO

I am Graciela Daleo. At present I am a member of the Disappeared Detainees' Association and during the military dictatorship, precisely when the 1978 World Cup was going on, I had disappeared into the Mechanical School of the Army, the ESMA. I had been kidnapped in October 1977 as a result of my political activity: I am a militant, had been a militant in revolutionary Peronism since 1967.

The issue of the 1978 World Cup was in fact an issue which we discussed quite a lot within the popular movements, even during the dictatorship. The 1976 coup took place on 24 March. By then, it had already been established that Argentina would be the host nation and practically any kind of militancy, whether student, unionist, revolutionary or political, was a clandestine activity. Even so, in those circles, we discussed what to do with the World Cup when it arrived. Both in Argentina and among the *companeros* who had managed to leave the country whether or not to boycott the event was heavily debated. When I say we discussed this I mean we discussed it within the very difficult and precarious conditions within which we had to discuss everything. It was perhaps more openly debated among exiled Argentines. Here, in Argentina, we were much more concerned with another type of situation, of survival and of attempting to articulate some sort of resistance. But the World Cup issue was always present, as was the issue of what attitude should be adopted towards the event. My personal opinion is that we ought to have developed a much stronger move towards denouncing what the 1978 World Cup would mean for Argentina. The counterargument was that the World Cup would provide an opportunity for the world's press to tell the world what was happening in the country. I must confess I was never persuaded by this argument because I believed a different type of attitude could have been more powerful; to encourage and promote the idea in the rest of the world that the teams shouldn't come, or that they should adopt a more critical attitude like I think the Dutch did. The Dutch came, but nevertheless they adopted a much more critical posture in the face of what was going on in the country.

And I think this situation was always loaded with something which has still not been resolved and which is becoming an increasingly serious problem: how to reconcile the importance of participating and respecting something which is a very strong popular feeling, such as football, on the one hand, and on the other how to confront power even through the relationship with sport. I think this is an unresolved issue and it can be quite unfriendly, or distasteful, within popular organisations because one runs the risk of being told, like I was, 'your problem is that you intellectualise everything because you don't like football'.

I was kidnapped in October 1977 and the World Cup happened during the month of June 1978, which means I had been in the concentration camp for eight months. Perhaps the best definition of 'being disappeared' is given by the word our kidnappers used to refer to us: they didn't talk of 'kidnapping' they talked of 'sucking'. And they referred to those of us who were in concentration camps not as disappeared or kidnapped but as 'sucked ones'. And the sound meant by being grabbed from the street and no one ever hearing from you again is 'SSHRUP'. It's the sound of a body falling into water and the body can no longer be seen, it disappears from the surface. To a large extent it was that. The surface returns to what it was like before, for a little while the circles which are formed remain, and then it goes back to what it was. And inside that mass, and those who look in from the outside can't see, well inside that, underneath that – that's where we were.

This means neither your family, nor your friends, nor the organisation or group you were a member of, nor the judiciary power had it been interested in knowing what was happening to us, knew anything about where we were. We had disappeared. That's what it was. The word disappeared means no longer being, no longer being anywhere. Although *we were* somewhere, and that somewhere was in concentration camps controlled by the Armed Forces. When one says no longer being it is because to some extent you are to the extent that others know you are – can see you and know you are there. That's what was not happening in Argentina.

I was kidnapped in a subway station and while I was being kidnapped the people around me at the station tried to help me. They couldn't because many armed men scared them off with threats – that the same as was being done to me would be done to them. As I was dragged up the stairs, the sensation that remains with me is that I was pulled into a car and everything returned to how it was before. Each person in the underground must have gone on to the office, some maybe told what happened and others will have remained silent because it was fear that caused the most damage in Argentina, and silence covered everything. The circles on the water stilled, everything continued.

There were things common to the entire repression, but there were also peculiarities of each concentration camp. The thing about the ESMA is that there the horror characteristic of the repression as a whole had certain sophistications which it would be too lengthy to describe now, but among them was the fact that task force 3.3/2, the commanding task force of that camp, decided to select a group of prisoners, of disappeared, to rehearse with them what they called 'a process of recuperation'. A simple way of putting it would be to say it was the Navy's attempt at brainwashing.

I was one of the prisoners selected for the process of recuperation. This meant that instead of spending twenty-four hours a day every day until I heard my number called out, on one of those Wednesdays when prisoners were transferred in order to be assassinated by being thrown alive into the sea, instead of this there was a group of prisoners who spent part of the day handcuffed and hooded, then some time with no handcuffs, then some time with no hood, and part of the time in another area of the concentration camp known as the fishtank. Here, a series of activities took place for which prisoners were utilised as slave labour. In my particular case, I was a typist. That was my skill anyway, and I was very fast, this elemental ability for any kind of secretarial job was viewed as a bizarre phenomenon by the marines who found it difficult to press one key after another. To give you an idea of what kind of things I typed, other prisoners selected like I had been for the process of recuperation would be asked for research and reports; one of them had to do an analysis of the history of the Beagle Channel – an issue at the time as there was a border dispute going on with Chile; another was ordered to prepare an article which was later used by the Chief of Intelligence's brother as his own coursework at War School. We were ordered to do these kind of things, and I typed them up.

This is by way of an explanation as to why during the World Cup those of us who were undergoing the process of recuperation watched the World Cup matches on TV. In a sense, part of the process of recuperation, or the methodology involved in that process, was about deconstructing us as people and building us up again following what they called 'western and Christian values'.

We could conclude that what the marines were rehearsing on us is what they intended to do with society as a whole. Using certain methodologies where the central thing was terror, and an economic void, and a certain form of psychological action, their aim was to rebuild a totally different society in order to create the Argentina we have now.

Therefore, there was a TV set in the fishtank, and we, the disappeared, watched the games. And here, as in the outside, a contradictory process was taking place, and this may seem paradoxical, because we watched the games and got excited or angry or suffered internally as the match progressed but at the same time – and this is something we couldn't say – we couldn't get it out of our heads that while the cameras showed us Massera, Videla and Agosti shouting the goals what was happening, even to us, was going on. And what's even more terrifying, the River stadium that was one of the World Cup venues, is very near the ESMA so every time there was a goal scored there the prisoners, those who did spend twenty-four hours a day hooded and handcuffed, and who in some cases spent seven, eight or even nine months in those conditions until they were assassinated, there, in the tenebrosity of the hood and in that silence, they heard the goals scored at River.

And for the *companeros* who were lying 'in the hood' all the time, the World Cup, through those sounds and the conversations of the guards, became a topic of interest. This is absolutely paradoxical.

Well, that's how the World Cup took place. There was an added problem that increased the horror of this which was the fact that the Navy had concluded and gathered some information about some revolutionary movements, mostly Montoneros, planning to send people into Argentina precisely to take advantage of the presence of so much press and to denounce what was happening here. So they were very alert and all the borders were controlled much more thoroughly and specifically than previously. So the World Cup brought this added pain of knowing that more *companeros* would fall because we knew the network – we knew inside the camp but we had no way of warning anyone – the network to suck militants was stronger than ever. This was another terrible aspect of the World Cup, it represented enhanced danger for those who wanted to come to Argentina to denounce what was happening.

I think by describing what I'm now going to describe I can express the clearest and deepest experience of those days, and it's the day the World Cup ended. The day the World Cup ended all the prisoners undergoing this supposed recuperation were in a little room at the back of the fishtank where the TV was. We were all there watching the game. The game finished with Argentina's triumph, we all hugged each other with this ambivalence I was talking about earlier – that sort of happiness on the one hand which we expressed and manifested because we genuinely felt it and also that desperate and terrible knowledge of what all that meant. We were doing this and the Chief of Intelligence of the ESMA, whose name still today absolutely terrifies me, Captain Jorge Eduardo Acosta, the sinister inventor of great part of the entire machinery, came up to the third floor which is where the fishtank was and hugged all of us one by one. He came in shouting 'We won! We won!' He shook the men's hands and kissed the women. And what I felt then was: if he's won, we've lost. There is nothing we can have in common. If for him this is a victory, then for us it is a defeat.

After that a guard came up with a list and told us 'get ready to go out'. I was one of the people on that list of five or six, I can't remember how many. There were some cars waiting, I remember I went in a green Peugeot 504. I remember it to this day. It was driven by an officer, Alberto Mendoza, and commanding this operation was Prefect Hector Antonio Febres, who was in charge of pregnant prisoners and of placing the babies born in concentration camps. I was taken in that car and we drove up the avenue. We were a column of cars heading towards Cabildo Avenue, and we headed towards Juramento Street, towards town. I was amazed by the amount of people in the street. People came out of their houses and proceeded up the avenue in the way one always had dreamt would be the day of liberation, the day of the triumph and the revolution. Our dream of militants. Well, people were coming out simply to celebrate a World Cup.

At one point I asked if they would allow me to stand up, and lean out of the roof of the car. They said yes so I stood up and I couldn't believe what I was seeing; rivers and rivers of people singing. And I burst into tears because I thought, if I start shouting now 'I'm disappeared' no one is going to pay any notice. I think it was one of the most tangible examples of the surface remaining the same and of us not having a real existence.

Anyway, as the amount of people on Cabildo Avenue was so enormous, cars couldn't move. So they decided to take us to a restaurant for a meal. The column of cars turned round, and headed towards Martinez neighbourhood, to a grill I had visited many times as a militant because we had thought it was a safe place. It too was completely packed, and we were led – us, an apparently normal group of men and women celebrating the World Cup – to a very large table where we were sat all together, torturers with prisoners. The guy who had tortured you with electric drills some time ago was now sharing the same table sitting next to you, and as everyone did we sang the songs of victory and celebrated. At one point I felt I could no longer tolerate this act (a large part of the time I spent disappeared was a huge act for me, acting as if I was susceptible to this process of recuperation) and I asked for permission to go to the bathroom. One way of showing that the process of recuperation was going ahead successfully, with the women, was to give us make-up often stolen or confiscated from other *companeras* – it was assumed women were politically active because we were unattractive or because men didn't fancy us and one of the indications that we were recuperating was to worry about our appearance – so I had some lipstick in my handbag. I locked myself into the WC, holding the door, and I graffitied the walls with my lipstick 'Military assassins, Massera son of a bitch, long live the montoneros'. When I had no lipstick left I went out of the WC, went back to the table and sat down again. It was a small gesture of freedom which relieved me of the anguish and despair momentarily, but as soon as I sat down at the table again I started to feel terror – even today this is one of the most terrifying feelings; this sensation that they are everywhere – I started to think 'what if they go into the bathroom after me and notice that the lipstick on the wall is the same colour I'm wearing?' That didn't happen and when we finished our meal we returned to the concentration camp.

I don't remember any of the songs now, but we sang them all. This thing of a parallel world was a permanent issue. We sang, and we were singing, but it was as if we had many tracks inside. As you sing part of you is genuinely singing and there's another part of you that isn't, this part that can stand back and observe, and becomes horrified with what it's seeing. I tell you, it is not dissimilar to the risk of madness. At least that's how I lived it. Other *companeros* maybe . . . the time of the World Cup maybe for the male *companeros*, maybe it had more to do with them. I don't know, the football thing becomes the dominating thing even in the concentration camp. The torturer who had tortured you when you were kidnapped, if he supported the same club as you did, this terribly mad ghostly bond would be established.

Whenever I hear that song by Serrat, 'Fiesta', where he sings 'the villain and the rich man shake hands, the differences don't matter' . . . I don't know. I've got an anger that has less to do with a sociological analysis and is more a gut reaction: I hate World Cups because they dissolve the class struggle. In a way, during the World Cup it seems we are all the same. We are not all the same.

The criticism thrown at me has always been that I don't understand football, that football is a party and all this stuff. I can't see it this way.

I would like to add something so as not to be unfair to my *companeros*. I remember one guy, Andres Castillo, who was a fanatical River fan, absolutely fanatical, and the torturer and assassin Juan Carlos Rolon was also a River fan so they enjoyed this detailed exchange. They would remember, I don't know, the first goal scored by the first River team, anyway I remember Andres, though he devoured each and every one of the games, refused to watch the inaugural ceremony. Which I did see. I sat in front of the TV and watched. And when Andres came to the fishtank later and I asked him why he had chosen to remain in the hood he said 'because I can't watch that'. To him that was a circus, he loved the football but the ceremonial stuff he wouldn't watch. And I also remember something we were all silently concerned with and worried about; there was a big question mark over whether the players, once the final was over, whether they would or wouldn't shake hands with the military. This was a big worry at the time and now I can't remember what happened. I remember the Cup, and then there's a blank.

When Argentina lost to Cameroon in the opening game in 1990, I was so pleased. I was pleased mostly because Cameroon are an African country, and I felt it was a victory for the Third World. And then I thought, maybe in Cameroon there is some terrible dictatorship going on, some ghastly government manipulating this football game (I ought to know what kind of government was in power at the time) and I wasn't so sure about being happy they had won anymore.

This is an unedited transcript of Graciela Daleo's oral account of her own experience of the 1978 World Cup, as told to Marcela Mora y Araujo and Tom Watt in an interview for BBC Radio Five Live.

Translated by Marcela Mora y Araujo.

oasis

MARK FISH

The place I envision
has the transparency of the Mediterranean
the beauty of the once before Amazon
It's yours and mine to share.
I am your ambassador
I'll show you this oasis
Where our skin can touch like the grass
our minds embedded together as the clouds in the sky.
This place has no limitations
together we are inseparable
the more time we are together
the stronger we become as one.

home support

IAN MCMILLAN

It is mid-July, 1997, It is hot.
Barnsley are in the Premier League,
and in my head our season
is laid out as simple as an Underground Map,
or a child's drawing of the solar system,
Mid-July, a pre-season friendly
against Doncaster. The start of something
and one of my daughters is coming to Doncaster
on her own for the first time on the bus
to meet me to go to the match. As the bus
rolls into the bus station I see her red shirt
upstairs, and she waves, and my heart breaks

for her, and me, and her red shirt with 21 TINKLER
on the back, and the bus driver who is a Middlesbrough fan,
and the other people who tumble off the bus in their red shirts
with the season laid out in their heads simple and lovely
as a map of the solar system or a child's drawing
of the Underground, and the Greek bus station toilet attendant
who knows me and shouts PREMIER LEAGUE, but
mostly it breaks for her, and me, and her red shirt.

Still, it's July. It's hot. We meet Chris and Duncan
and we try to go into a pub even though my daughter's
a bit young and a man in a suit says Sorry, Home Support Only.
And my heart breaks

for her, and me, and her red shirt, and the Home Support
who cheer Doncaster and whose season is laid out simple
as a serving suggestion, or a child's drawing of a football team,
but mostly it breaks for her and me.

We get a taxi home, which seems extravagant, but I think
of the Greek toilet attendant and I shout PREMIER LEAGUE
on our path as we walk into the house, father and daughter,
red shirt, hot night, Home Support, season laid out in our heads
simple and lovely as a football programme, simple and lovely
as a penalty kick, a well-taken corner.

tony adams

HENK SPAAN

Sick boy he is not
Nor Rents, Spud or Second Prize
But in Begbie's bunch of
Baseball Bats, the
Hollow eyes, skins tight
Over cheekbones.
For them there's little hope
Teeth gone or black and rotting.
Irvine Welsh no doubt
Had seen him when
He wrote his *Trainspotting*.

I feel all icky

the contributors

Gabriel 'Batigol' Batistuta has scored more goals for Argentina than Diego Maradona, and that means more than anyone else. His autobiography – an autobiography in the sense that he wrote it himself – has been nominated for an Italian literary prize.

Hugo Borst, the Dennis Bergkamp of Dutch football writing, is no longer on speaking terms with Ed de Goey. If you are reading this, Ed, Hugo is sorry for whatever he did.

Liz Crolley, an academic at Manchester Metropolitan University, is the author of several books on football and has not missed a Liverpool home game in 20 years.

Graciela Daleo is a member of Asociacion Detenidos Desaparecidos in Buenos Aires, a support group for survivors of concentration camps which lobbies for the reconstruction of collective history and memory. In 1989, the first democratic government in Argentina since the military coup of 1976 tried and subsequently pardoned all those involved in the so-called 'dirty war', both military oppressors and members of armed guerrilla groups. Of all those tried and pardoned, Graciela Daleo was the only one who rejected the pardon.

Paul Davis is an artist and illustrator and was once voted *Marie Claire* man of the month.

Mark Fish is a prominent young South African poet who also plays football for his country.

Gordon Henderson is an American non-mainstream artist. He is the author of the ten-story Chicken Gimlet cycle – billed in the promotional literature as the 'bedtime story you may never wake up from'. Need we say anything more? His yearly cartoon calendars have been an international hit since the 1980s.

Guus van Holland writes for the Dutch newspaper *NRC Handelsblad*. So good they named the country after him.

Simon Hughes played cricket for Middlesex, football for his college at Durham University, and won the William Hill Award for Sports Book of the Year in 1997 with *A Lot of Hard Yakka*. Football is not his thing.

Roger Hutchinson wrote *It Is Now!* (about the 1966 World Cup, obviously) and *The Toon* (about Newcastle United, of course). He lives somewhere in Scotland.

Simon Inglis is remaking himself as a man who no longer writes about football grounds, unless it is for huge amounts of money.

Simon Kuper is a *Financial Times* journalist and author of *Football Against the Enemy*.

Ian McMillan is poet-in-residence at Barnsley FC. We hope you like his poem. He's pleased with it. So are we.

Julia Napier grew up in Atlanta, but as a facet of the globalisation phenomenon now lives in Buenos Aires. Although still in her early twenties, she is a former top-class footballer. One of the leading poets of the twenty-first century.

Rob Newman, stand-up comedian turned award-winning novelist, his latest novel, *Manners*, is published on the same day as this book.

Joseph O'Connor is English through and through. No, that was a joke. Joseph O'Connor is an Irish novelist and journalist whose books include *The Irish Male At Home and Abroad*, *The Secret World of the Irish Male*, *Cowboys and Indians* and *Desperadoes*. Football is not his thing.

Amy Raphael's interview with Courtney Love (the first after Kurt Cobain killed himself) appeared in her book *Never Mind the Bollocks: Women Rewrite Rock*. The sequel will be called *Never Mind the Balls: Rock Stars Rewrite Football*. She is sports editor at *Esquire*.

Harry Ritchie, tall, own hair, well hung, considered intelligent. GSOH, seeks footballing woman or similar.

Without *Henk Spaan*, *Perfect Pitch* would never have existed. Henk set up *Hard Gras*, the Dutch literary football magazine from which we stole the idea. He is also a poet, a television comedian whose impressions of Pope John Paul II are legendary, and the best host in Amsterdam. Give him a call next time you are there.

Still Available

perfect pitch

1) home ground

EDITED BY
SIMON KUPER

The best new football writing, featuring:

Dannie Abse on sixty-four years as a Cardiff City fan.

James Wilson visits Faustino Asprilla in Colombia and Newcastle.

Hugo Borst, Holland's best football writer, on the tragic
Van Basten family.

Jim White on our lives after Cantona.

Karl Miller chastises the referees.

Simon Kuper meets Bert Trautmann during Euro 96.

Emma Lindsey studies life as a footballer's wife.

Jimmy Burns describes how writing a biography of Diego Maradona
caused him to disintegrate.

D.J. Taylor makes an imaginary visit to Hackney Marshes; and on
the place of football in English literature.

Jorge Valdano, a World Cup winner, on a small pitch.

Simon Veksner on the Battle of Wounded Knee.

'An excellent buy' *Express*

'Ideally suited to fill a gap in the market for creative writing about
our most popular sport' *Independent*

'With the exception of *Perfect Pitch* we don't get a single publication
devoted to seriously good sports writing' *Irish Times*

'An enormously promising idea . . . *Perfect Pitch* should prosper
mightily if these standards are maintained' *Pete Davies*

NON-FICTION / SPORT 0 7472 7698 6
Price £7.99 Available from all good bookshops

Still Available

perfect pitch

2) foreign field

EDITED BY
SIMON KUPER

The best new writing on football featuring:

Blake Morrison on the memoirs of Ian and Billy Wright.
Patrick Barclay looks forward to when Scotland win the World Cup.
Frans Oosterwijk on Ronaldo, the world's greatest player.
Simon Inglis on an emotional trip to a football match.
Hugo Borst on Dennis Bergkamp.
Marcela Mora y Araujo joins Gary Lineker in Argentina.
Lynne Truss on what might have happened in the World Cup.
Harry Ritchie and the famous Tartan Army.
Joe Boyle on the rage of Giggs.
Stuart Ford, who wore Three Lions on his shirt.
Simon Veksner on every fan's dream.
Nicholas Royle is Desperately Seeking Euclid.
D.J. Taylor remembers The Nest.
Luis Fernando Verissimo on Brazilian life.

'Another superb collection' *Sunday Times*
'This is a wonderful, wonderful book; at long last, football writing
that can be read on the train without embarrassment' *FourFourTwo*
'Pin-sharp snapshots from Planet Football' *The Times*
'Just another football book rather like Johan Cruyff was just another
player' *Maxim*

NON-FICTION / SPORT 0 7472 7697 8
Price £7.99 Available from all good bookshops

perfect pitch

4) dirt

EDITED BY SIMON KUPER and
MARCELA MORA Y ARAUJO

will be published on 8 April 1999 (ISBN 0 7472 7511 4)
in Review softback, on a theme of 'dirt', and whether it can be
found in football. Among those who will be writing for this
fourth edition are:

Gabriel Batistuta
Hugo Borst
Simon Buckby
Jimmy Burns
David Conn
Phil Crossley
Hunter Davies
Roddy Doyle
Ceri Evans
Simon Inglis
Rob Newman
Amy Raphael
D.J. Taylor
Lynne Truss
Simon Veksner
James Wilson
Marguerite Yourcenar

Further contributors will follow.